Corporate Governance and Control

edited by

Alex Dunlop

Sheffield Hallam University

D0319359

The Chartered Institute of Management Accountants

Editor's note

This book has been edited and adapted from the CIMA Management Accounting Control Systems *Knowledge* text from the CIMA Study and Revision Pack, written by John Williams. His permission for the use of this material is gratefully acknowledged.

Copyright © CIMA 1998
First published in 1998 by:
The Chartered Institute of Management Accountants
63 Portland Place
London
W1N 4AB

ISBN 0 7494 2683 7

Contents

Introduction

There has never been a time when systems of corporate governance and control have been under greater scrutiny than they currently are. The need for effective and efficient procedures is high on the agenda of companies and other organisations around the world.

The reasons for this are not difficult to trace. In the late 1980s investors and commentators were confronted by many large-scale business failures and executive remuneration excess in the UK, capital market abuses in the USA and corporate and political fraud in Japan. This situation has been heightened as we move through the current decade by the ever-increasing pace of change and the growing complexity and sophistication of business arrangements and financial transactions, facilitated by the pervasive power of information technology.

It is virtually impossible, however, to devise a system of governance and control which will satisfy completely the multifarious requirements frequently demanded of it. Indeed, institutions which have invested huge amounts of money in establishing high-level compliance and control systems have frequently been shocked to discover that substantial sums have either been lost through imprudent, speculative or erroneous trading or have simply been fraudulently misappropriated.

That is not to say that such systems were totally ineffectual – the very nature of the reporting of these cases is usually negative. It is the horror stories which attract the most readers. The positive aspects, i.e. the scale of the successful prevention of such events by the same systems, are never mentioned. Like any other business system, governance and control has to be cost-effective; it has to produce more benefits than the cost of the time and effort involved in establishing it. It has to be appropriate for the particular circumstances with which it has to cope and even the smallest companies and organisations can benefit from having suitably scaled procedures in the first place.

The aspects and areas of corporate life which can benefit from the presence of governance and control systems and procedures are generally felt to be:

1   **Board arrangements**. Remit and operational details; roles and responsibilities of the chairman and of the chief executive; policies concerning the use and appointment of non-executive directors; formation and role of the audit committee.
2   **Executive remuneration**. Policy, development, operation and monitoring.
3   **Environmental, ethical, health and safety and employment matters**. Policy development, monitoring systems, extent and method of public disclosure.

4 **Systems for risk assessment and internal control.** Development, implementation, review (including internal audit or independent review), reporting structures and follow-up.

Each of these areas is referred to in this book, with the intention of providing some degree of insight and practical assistance to readers from all sizes of companies and other organisations.

1 Corporate Governance

Corporate governance involves the quality assurance of the operation of the board itself. Sheridan and Kendall (1992) said:

> 'Management is concerned with the company's operations, governance with ensuring that the executives do their jobs properly.' (page 146)

There are several different models of how corporate governance can be implemented within a company and two are discussed here. Corporate governance is widely regarded as the evaluation of the performance of the executive directors of the company by, or for, the company stakeholders. These include shareholders, employees, banks, and creditors. The extent to which all stakeholders should be involved differs between commentators. The clear German/European model is for the involvement of all these stakeholders mentioned, whereas the current UK model involves a smaller number of stakeholders.

The first model of corporate governance implementation is often regarded as the ideal model and involves three groups of participants at director level. These include the *executive board* which is appointed by the shareholders to run the company, the *supervisory board* appointed by stakeholders including employees, bankers, etc., and the *advisory board* which consists of independent experts brought into the company to provide technical and external expertise to assist the company.

The executive and supervisory boards together form the board of directors of the company; the advisory board, on the other hand, may sit separately or with the board of directors. Under current UK law these three groups can only form a common unitary board (though on the continent of Europe it is possible for the supervisory board to exist separately from the executive board). The advisory board need not be a board at all in that its members may not need to be part of the legal board of directors. Under this particular structure, the job of corporate governance is undertaken by the supervisory board and they may have an agenda which consists of the following items:

- appraising the executive board;
- overseeing compliance;
- watching out for trouble and preparing for it;
- overseeing and controlling the pension fund arrangements.

(Sheridan and Kendall, page 150)

Figure 1.1: An 'ideal' board structure for corporate governance

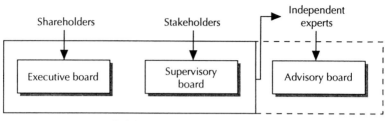

Board of directors

The UK pattern is different. There is a unitary board – and all directors have equal legal liability, and are all responsible for the company. Divisions of the board into executive and non-executive directors, or the formation of committees of the board, such as the audit committee, do not affect the legal position.

1.1 The aims of reform of corporate governance

The problem could be defined as one of ensuring that the directors or those managing the company act in the interests of the shareholders, or, in the way the debate has developed, the directors act in the interests of all those to whom they owe duties, or the stakeholders.

This could be explained as the progressive development of company law, and in particular the law relating to company accounts and their audit. This law could be regarded as delineating constitutional relationships between directors, shareholders, and auditors – relationships which needed to be rewritten from time to time as it became apparent from a succession of frauds that the previous law provided inadequate protection against directors. The original concept was that of stewardship, directors managing assets on shareholders' behalf, and accounting to them for the assets in their custody.

Viewed in this way, the development of company law is the development of ever more complex regulation of companies, with which the vast majority of companies have complied, but which has been unable to prevent recurring scandals. There is considerable difficulty in attempting to legislate for every possibility, and a significant cost to those who comply.

However, it would be mistaken to look at the subject in such a narrow way. The range of ways of approaching the control problem explain the difficulties in trying to find solutions, and even in defining the problem.

The aims of proposed reforms of corporate governance have to be considered in an international context in that, very broadly, similar developments have taken place in several countries. Change in the UK, with its emphasis on non-legislative approaches, is most closely paralleled by change in the USA, where the Treadway Report was produced by COSO (Committee of Sponsoring Organisations, 1991). The UK history of the development of large firms, and their legal and financial structure, is similar to that of the USA, but quite different from that in Germany and Japan.

Within the EU, there has been more emphasis on the need for uniform practices as part of the implementation of the single market. There have also been difficulties because much of the change to date in the EU has concerned worker participation in company management and governance, exemplified by works councils, and in many countries worker representation on boards. So far, this has had only limited effects in the UK, because of the Maastricht treaty opt-out by the UK from the Social Chapter. The new Labour government has, however, expressed its intention that the UK should become a party to it.

At this broad level the aims could be explained in a range of ways:

- creating a framework for the control of large powerful companies whose interests may not coincide with the national interest;
- controlling multinationals which can dominate the local economy;
- ensuring that companies are answerable to all stakeholders, not just to shareholders;
- ensuring that companies are run according to the laws and standards of the country, and are not in effect 'states within states';
- ensuring that companies behave in a socially responsible way; this could cover matters as diverse as environmental concerns, equal opportunities, support for the arts and other good causes, regional development and employment;
- protecting investors, who buy shares, in the same way as investors who buy any other financial investment product, such as insurance or a pension, are protected.

These approaches, seen as political aims, are not necessarily compatible with a free markets approach – that companies can arrange their own affairs as they wish, subject to the minimum necessary legal framework. No comment is implied on the merits of these aims, or on their relative priority. No possible structure for corporate governance will meet all aims.

The difficult problem of practical and political issues is well illustrated by the problem of employee participation. This is legally established in many European countries and there is considerable political debate on the extension of such systems to the UK as part of the European Union Social Chapter. There is scope for political debate about whether such compulsory establishment is desirable. Apart from the political issues, there are practical issues such as the actual working of these systems:

- in many European countries systems of employee participation have worked for many years including employee representatives on boards;
- many major UK companies have established such systems on a voluntary basis.

1.2 The Cadbury Report

The Cadbury Committee (the Committee on the Financial Aspects of Corporate Governance) was established in 1991 by the London Stock Exchange, the Financial Reporting Council, and the accountancy profession, which were concerned at the lack of confidence in financial reporting. It was not a government-appointed commission, and was never envisaged as recommending legislation. This arises from the then government having a firm belief in self-regulation, within a broad statutory framework, being the way to provide the minimum protection necessary for investors (and possibly other stakeholders), without inhibiting market forces. It also reflected the difficulty for the government of finding legislative time to debate a possibly complex set of measures.

Cadbury aimed to put forward practical ways of raising financial control and reporting standards, which could be put into effect without waiting for legislation. This excluded a UK SEC (Securities and Exchange Commission) with legal powers on the USA pattern. A different government could well take the view that legislation is more appropriate, and would certainly threaten legislation if it did not broadly approve of the approach taken.

The Cadbury Committee had a fairly narrow remit: the financial aspects of corporate governance, not corporate governance itself. This apparently excluded radical approaches such as two-tier boards and worker representatives, but the thinking was clearly influenced by the apparent success of the German model.

The general approach was to make recommendations based on current perceived best practice in the hope of achieving consensus and voluntary acceptance. There was the view that better governance would lead to better economic performance.

Increasing disclosure was seen to be crucial in maintaining public trust in the corporate system, and a key part of raising standards. It could be seen as a means of encouraging effective shareholder (and stakeholder) interest – checks and balances against professional managers.

Strengthening the influence of shareholders is also important as a check on directors, but this is difficult to achieve within a financial system where the proportion of shares in public companies held directly by individuals has fallen considerably compared with the shares held indirectly by individuals through pension funds, and unit and investment trusts. Institutional shareholders, though now changing significantly, have been reluctant to become too involved in company affairs when unhappy, preferring to sell shares than to propose change.

The main emphasis has been on defining and changing the way in which the board ought to work – building necessary checks and balances into board structures. This would help prevent a domineering chief executive indulging in vendettas, defrauding the company, or following a policy for personal rather than logical commercial reasons.

Specific Cadbury proposals

The Committee reported in 1992. A Code of Best Practice, embodying underlying principles of openness, integrity, and accountability, was put forward and is reproduced below.

Figure 1.2: Cadbury Committee – Code of Best Practice

1 *The board of directors*

1.1 The board should meet regularly, retain full and effective control over the company and monitor the executive management.

1.2 There should be a clearly accepted division of responsibilities at the head of the company, which will ensure a balance of power and authority, such that no one individual has unfettered powers of decision. Where the chairman is also the chief executive, it is essential that there should be a strong and independent element on the board, with a recognised senior member.

1.3 The board should include non-executive directors of sufficient calibre and number for their views to carry significant weight in the board's decision.

1.4 The board should have a formal schedule of matters specifically reserved to it for decision to ensure that direction and control of the company is firmly in its hands.

1.5 There should be an agreed procedure for directors in the furtherance of their duties to take independent professional advice if necessary, at the company's expense.

1.6 All directors should have access to the advice and services of the company secretary, who is responsible to the board for ensuring that board procedures are followed and that applicable rules and regulations are complied with. Any question of the removal of the company secretary should be a matter for the board as a whole.

2 *Non-executive directors*

2.1 Non-executive directors should bring an independent judgement to bear on issues of strategy, performance, resources, including key appointments, and standards of conduct.

2.2 The majority should be independent of management and free from any business or other relationship which could materially interfere with the exercise of their independent judgement, apart from their fees and shareholding. Their fees should reflect the time which they commit to the company.

2.3 Non-executive directors should be appointed for specified terms and reappointment should not be automatic.

2.4 Non-executive directors should be selected through a formal process and both this process and their appointment should be a matter for the board as a whole.

3 *Executive directors*

3.1 Directors' service contracts should not exceed three years without shareholders' approval.

3.2 There should be full and clear disclosure of directors' total emoluments and those of the chairman and highest-paid UK director, including pension contributions and stock options. Separate figures should be given for salary and performance-related elements and the basis on which performance is measured should be explained.

Continued...

3.3 Executive directors' pay should be subject to the recommendations of a remuneration committee made up wholly of or mainly of non-executive directors.

4 Reporting and controls

4.1 It is the board's duty to present a balanced and understandable assessment of the company's position.

4.2 The board should ensure that an objective and professional relationship is maintained with the auditors.

4.3 The board should establish an audit committee of at least three non-executive directors with written terms of reference which deal clearly with its authority and duties.

4.4 The directors should explain their responsibility for preparing the accounts next to a statement by the auditors about their reporting responsibilities.

4.5 The directors should report on the effectiveness of the company's internal control.

4.6 The directors should report that the business is a going concern, with supporting assumptions or qualifications as necessary.

Source: *Report of the Committee on the Financial Aspects of Corporate Governance*, 1992

This contained recommendations for:

▪ the conduct of the board of directors; regular meetings, division of responsibilities at the head of the company so that ideally the chairman is not also the chief executive, reservation of powers to the board to ensure control, provision for directors to take independent legal advice, and the responsibility of the company secretary to ensure that board procedures are followed;

▪ a significant number of non-executive directors should be formally selected by the board as a whole and should be independent of management and from any relationships with the company. They should be appointed for specified terms and should bring an independent judgement to issues of strategy, performance, key appointments, and standards of conduct;

▪ executive directors' contracts should not exceed three years without shareholders' approval. Total emoluments should be subject to the recommendations of a remuneration committee which would wholly or mainly consist of non-executive directors. The emoluments should be fully disclosed;

▪ the board have the duty to present a balanced and understandable assessment of the company position. An audit committee of at least three non-executive directors should be established;

▪ the directors should report on the effectiveness of internal control and that the business is a going concern, subject, for both these requirements, to the issue of guidance for directors and auditors.

The London Stock Exchange has adopted as part of its listing rules the requirement for listed companies, if incorporated in the UK, to report whether they have complied with the Code. This is a requirement to report on compliance or non-compliance – not a requirement to comply with the recommendations.

1.3 Greenbury and reporting on directors' remuneration

Following concern regarding pay levels at the top of privatised utilities, and a general greater political concern in the UK than other countries with issues of inequality, the Greenbury Committee was appointed to review the arrangements for paying directors and to make appropriate recommendations.

This committee reported in July 1995, going further than Cadbury in some significant respects, and compliance has been made a listing requirement by the Stock Exchange.

The key requirements are:

- the remuneration committee (already part of the Cadbury Code) should consist entirely of non-executive directors 'with no personal financial interest other than as shareholders in the matters to be decided'. This has caused considerable adverse comment from some public company chief executives who regard it as their responsibility to fix the pay of other directors, and that moving this responsibility to other, non-executive, directors would weaken the position of the chief executive;
- there should be no potential conflicts of interest from cross-directorships. The obvious example is when an executive director of X plc is a non-executive director of Y plc, and, at the same time, an executive director of Y plc is a non-executive director of X plc. They could both support higher pay for directors in both companies (i.e. for themselves) and could both be on remuneration committees as non-executive directors;
- there should be an annual report to shareholders, which may be approved by the annual general meeting.

It should be noted that disclosure of directors' remuneration is required by Cadbury. Greenbury has extended this to 'full transparency', detailing each individual director's remuneration in all its elements.

Directors' pensions
A case study in the problems of devising regulations

There have been considerable problems with regard to directors' pension entitlements, and how increases in these entitlements should be reported.

The problems arise because most UK pension schemes are related to the number of years of service and the final salary; in a generous scheme a pension-scheme member would retire after 40 years' salary on 40/60 of final salary.

If there is no exceptional salary increase beyond the normal adjustment for inflation, it could be argued that the problem of the adequacy of the pension fund to meet the increased claim on its resources is the same for the directors as for all other employees, and needs no special reporting.

But the problem that attracted public attention was that of the directors of privatised utilities, many of whom received substantial salary increases, virtually doubling their salaries, and hence their pension entitlement. Many were at late stages in their careers, and clearly would retire in a year or a few years. Normal employer and employee contributions to the pension scheme would be too small in the few years remaining to make any difference to the cost of the increased pension.

Assessing the adequacy of a pension fund to meet its obligations under a final salary scheme is a complex calculation requiring judgement over a very long period of anticipated inflation, anticipated return on investments, anticipated rates of salary increase in real terms, the proportion of employees who will leave before retirement, the lifespan of the retired and their dependents. The company, as ultimate guarantor, has to ensure that the fund is adequate, but the calculation, with all its sweeping assumptions, is normally only done triennially by the actuaries, after which the company may need to make an additional contribution, or may find that it can take a contribution holiday, and make no further contribution to the pension fund for a few years.

The original proposal from the Faculty of Actuaries was that, rather than attempt to do this complete calculation before and after any exceptional salary increase to a director, the capital value of the increased pension be calculated on the basis of the 'transfer value' if the director moved to another company and joined its pensions scheme. This would be quite easy to calculate – it is the discounted present value of the future income to the director, making appropriate assumptions, as made elsewhere in the pension fund calculations of potential lifespan and likely interest rates. Technically this was a sensible solution which identified the cost to the company, whether the cost was recognised in the current year or only in a triennial revaluation of the pension scheme, and involved, by pension standards, relatively few assumptions and a simple calculation. This calculation would be done frequently with leavers joining other companies and transferring to other pension schemes; with directors the sums would be larger.

Unfortunately, the system produces very large sums as answers.

A salary increase of, say, £100,000 for a director aged 59 and retiring at 60, would produce an increased pension of £60,000 p.a. if there had been 40 years of recognised service. The CBI (Confederation of British Industry) would like to disclose the figure of £60,000 p.a. which would be easily understood.

The actuaries would prefer to calculate the value of the £60,000 p.a. for the estimated lifespan (say to 77, the normal male lifespan), making appropriate assumptions re inflation, inflation adjustments to the pension, and interest rates. The answer could be well over £1,000,000 depending on the exact assumptions, and the shareholders could become very vociferous.

The current proposal is effectively that both methods be used, that the accrued pension benefit to the director be shown and either the transfer value shown or sufficient information disclosed to enable users of the accounts to make appropriate calculations.

The Greenbury Committee proceeded to make a series of recommendations which it wished companies to confirm they have considered, but which it was not prepared to make mandatory. These included:

- sensitivity to the wider pay scene, including pay and employment elsewhere in the company. This reflected current public concern at the scale of some top salaries;
- annual bonuses to be at least partly in shares to be held for a significant period. Shares granted should not have formal ownership and control transferred, or options granted be exercisable, for at least three years. Challenging performance criteria should be attached. Share options should not be issued at a discount. Institutional shareholders have shown considerable interest in this, and much activity in monitoring schemes which enable directors to earn shares for performance. Much of the problem of such schemes has been that the reward has been at best very loosely linked to controllable performance, and often the result of unexpected changes in the stock market. There has been a further problem that, while the option schemes have been disclosed, the cost of these schemes to the shareholders has not been apparent as, while it eventually affects earnings per share through the increased number of shares, there has been no charge to the profit and loss account;
- directors' contracts should be reduced in length, to one year or less. This reflected concern at high pay-offs – i.e. rewards for failure.

In practice it would probably be appropriate for the remuneration committee to consider the pay of senior managers along with the remuneration of executive directors, to ensure comparability.

The committee has provided little in the way of guidance to the wider pay scene, though it commented that the market in executive skills is imperfect, and that many directors spend much or all of their working lives with one company. As well as the market for executive skills, remuneration committees will have to consider:

- the need to provide adequate reward to encourage promotion at all levels in the company. With several layers of management, and differentials between all levels, top pay has to be high enough to permit adequate spacing of rewards to provide incentives to seek promotion;
- the ability of executives to move to another company, or to set up their own business, taking customers with them. This is particularly significant in people businesses such as advertising, and specialised financial services;
- the level of individual performance, possibly exceptional effort;
- the level of company performance.

These last two considerations take the role of the non-executive directors beyond providing a guarantee of ethical and transparent behaviour to shareholders. The non-executive directors are required to assess the executive directors – effectively placing them in charge in the long run.

Post-Greenbury reporting by public companies has had some unexpected consequences. Reports have revealed:

- a surprising diversity in practices in rewarding directors and in the level of security provided by contracts. Overall, levels of remuneration link only very loosely with obvious criteria such as company size or profitability;
- movements towards introducing long-term incentive plans do not appear to be leading to any reduction in basic pay or other forms of incentive. Greenbury could have been read as suggesting long-term incentive schemes as alternative ways of remunerating directors; many companies seem to regard them as additional remuneration;
- reporting of directors' remuneration has become remarkably voluminous. This leads to a number of questions:
  - are the code requirements so complex that the level of detail is needed to ensure compliance?
  - is the level of detail due to complex arrangements to remunerate directors, and are such complex arrrangements desirable or necessary? Did these complex arrangements arise from wishes to minimise tax, or from wishes to minimise disclosure to shareholders of the level of remuneration?

1.4 Corporate governance post-Cadbury

At the end of 1995 the successor committee to the Cadbury Committee (Cadbury II) was appointed under the chairmanship of Sir Ronald Hampel, the Chairman of ICI.

This committee has conducted a very wide-ranging review, and has examined the UK's present unitary board structure and considered whether it should be replaced by a two-tier structure, as in Germany. This would separate the management and supervisory functions of the board. There are clear difficulties with the Cadbury proposals which make non-executive directors responsible for monitoring the company and its management through audit and remuneration committees, but leave their legal responsibilities exactly the same as those of executive directors.

It has also considered the role of institutional shareholders in the selection of directors, and in corporate governance generally. A possible proposal is that they may be required to vote at general meetings, as American pension funds are obliged to.

Increasingly some of the larger institutional investors are moving away from the traditional way of influencing companies by informal contact towards establishing and publishing voting guidelines – declarations of how it will vote its shares on a range of issues of principle. Examples of this include the railway pension fund, which has policies for how its investment managers should vote on such matters as directors' contracts and dividend policy. Most have guidelines that broadly follow Cadbury and Greenbury.

The committee has also considered the Greenbury proposals for full disclosure and transparency on individual directors' pay. The area of particular difficulty is the cost of a pay increase to the pension fund, as discussed above.

In its interim report, published in the summer of 1997, the Hampel Committee has, however, adopted what appears to be a non-interventionist stance towards pushing forward further developments in systems of corporate governance. The report urges a flexible approach by shareholders and others in judging corporate governance best practice. The report says that shareholders should drop the so-called 'tick box' approach of checking compliance to rules and instead take account of the diversity of 'circumstances and experience among companies'.

This report has been subject to come degree of criticism from interested parties, mainly on the grounds of its apparent unwillingness to make specific recommendations in some important areas. For example, members of the Corporate Governance Forum, who represent the UK's leading fund management groups, have stated that, while there is much in Hampel to welcome, there are a number of omissions which are of concern. In particular, they argue that Hampel has failed to provide a definition of an independent non-executive director, nor listed examples of non-executives who are not independent. The committee has instead restated that it is for the board to decide in particular cases where the independence issue is blurred.

They also criticise the Hampel stance on directors being able to combine the roles of chairman and chief executive in that this could be seen as a green light to reversing the trend for separation of the roles. This point is picked up by the Institute of Chartered Secretaries and Administrators, which warns that the report's recommendation that companies appoint a lead non-executive director could harm boardroom relations; this has, in fact, the effect of undermining the committee's main non-separation recommendation.

Support for the committee has, however, come from the Institute of Chartered Accountants in England and Wales. The chairman of its corporate governance group, Sir Brian Jenkins, has said that implementation of the proposals would lead to substantial changes in the way directors were selected and the way financial information was presented. He added that the proposals would present a challenge to all.

The committee's final report, issued in January 1998, while endorsing key points from the Cadbury and Greenbury Reports, remains firmly in favour of evolutionary improvement to systems of corporate governance.

2 Control in Organisations

Control is an extremely wide concept, and any attempt to define or explain is liable to limit or restrict its scope in ways which will only later become apparent.

Achieving control can be a matter of quite complex systems and procedures in large organisations – but even with such structures it is immediately noticeable that control is effective in some organisations, but markedly less so in others – managers may neither know nor care regarding problems, and in any case do not have the authority to deal with them.

Some very small organisations can provide a sharp contrast. Control can appear total with everything watched, all decisions made and all expenditures made only by the sole owner manager. This example is a useful reminder that control is not about procedures and checklists – however useful these can be in assessment – but about the results achieved, about the effects of the process, however clear or unclear the nature of the process.

But even this very loose concept of control does not encompass the full meaning of the word, though it probably incorporates most of the range of possible meanings that it is desirable to discuss in this chapter.

This point is best explained by looking briefly at a few phrases in everyday usage. We can speak of someone as being or not being:

- 'in charge of his affairs';
- 'in charge of events';
- 'in charge of his destiny'.

The first phrase clearly describes the control of internal matters.

The second refers, at least in part, to the relationship between the organisation and other organisations and to internal processes. The external meaning is easily understood: a very small firm has little influence over customers or markets and must respond to their whims as well as to broad economic trends. This is the normal situation for a subcontractor or a supplier to a large chain store. Large firms can influence markets, and can even create new products and new markets. The internal meaning refers to the extent to which changes are anticipated and planned for. Some organisations are always surprised by changes in markets, in general economic circumstances, in the legal and regulatory environment, and are always reacting after the event to such changes. These tend to see all change as problematic, and are not looking for new opportunities. Others anticipate change, forecast possible consequences and adjust policy to minimise the adverse consequences and take advantage of new opportunities.

The third phrase refers to a set of very broad ideas, some of which are relevant, but most are quite beyond the scope of this section. The part that is relevant is the influence on organisations of societal consensus on how organisations and individuals ought to behave, and the question of how to understand this process. Examples of this are the way in which ideas have developed and been implemented to varying extents in different organisations and societies on such matters as acceptable commercial behaviour, equality of opportunity, social responsibility, and corporate governance. The ideas of Foucault are relevant here, the emphasis on processes of discipline, and the historical perspective on increasing control in all Western societies.

Most management accounting ideas of control start with the familiar cybernetic control model. Basic control models consist of analysing a simple input–process–output control loop as shown in Figure 2.1. Controls are necessary in this situation in order to keep a system operating within present tolerances. This basic model explains the use of feedback and feed-forward controls. Choice of the specific controls used depends on the reasons a system is likely to be out of control. Thus the controls must be to combat the reasons for being out of control (or risks) which a particular system faces. Interestingly, internal audit is itself a control because of the risk of a system's own internal controls not working properly.

Figure 2.1: A basic cybernetic control model

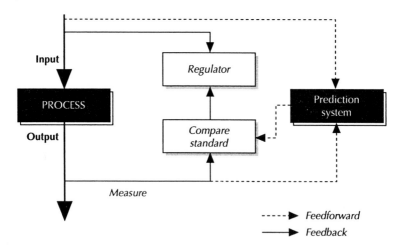

While these simple cybernetic control models are adequate to explain simple controls, more complex control models indicate a wider range of control functions and are more appropriate for some systems within a quality assurance framework. Figure 2.2 sets out one such framework and this suggests that control goes beyond the basic feedback and feedforward control into changing the *process*, the *objectives*, and the *predictive model of the system*, as appropriate. The wider framework of control is most appropriate for many types of quality assurance work as it suggests several actions that can be taken:

▪ change inputs (first-order control);

- amend objectives (second-order control);
- change the process (systematic learning);
- amend the model of the process (internal learning).

Figure 2.2: A more comprehensive control process

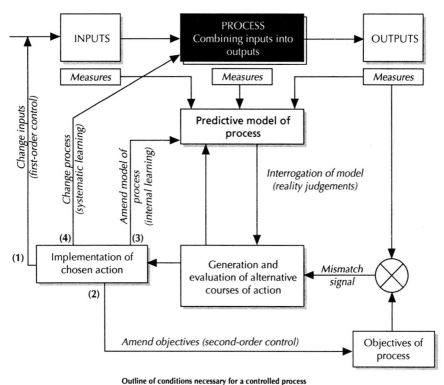

Outline of conditions necessary for a controlled process
Source: Otley and Berry, 'Control Organisation and Accounting', Accounting, Organisations and Society v5(2) pp231-244 (1980)

This framework is more realistic than the basic model but even this falls short of the complexity of the real world situation. It should also be noted that the implementation of internal controls, like other aspects of business, must be subject to cost-benefit analysis and this has led to the suggestion of the use of formal risk analysis.

The expanded cybernetic model demonstrates that the control process is more than a simple process within a self-contained organisation headed by management – the self-contained thermostat.

Defining the bounds of the organisation is not easy. For various purposes shareholders and stakeholders will have to be considered.

General ideas on the nature of control and acceptable forms of control will also need to be considered: one of the difficulties of the corporate governance debate is the extent to which there is a changed climate of opinion as well as a set of new specific requirements. This is easily illustrated by comparison. The requirements to report directors' earnings and entitlements are reasonably clear, and public companies can comply with a specific requirement, whether or not they accept the validity of the enquiry and any comparisons that might be made. There are no requirements (yet) to report on environmental issues, but many companies consider it appropriate to do so, even though they have no clear universally accepted basis for such reports – they are clearly influenced by the climate of opinion and anticipate that such reports will, sooner or later, become mandatory.

3 Internal Control

The importance of the Cadbury recommendation that directors should report on the effectiveness of internal control is that in effect it defines internal control as exercised by the board of the company, not just by the executive management, and implies a more general interest in its existence than that of the management, who would wish to see such a system as part of the process of management, ensuring that policy was properly implemented.

Internal control is remembered and defined by most in terms of the Auditing Practices Committee guideline on internal control issued in 1980, with its categorisation of eight types of internal control – even if most remember the various mnemonics rather than the list and its meaning.

The Auditing Practices Committee definition is:

> the whole system of controls, financial and otherwise, established by the management in order to carry on the business of the enterprise in an orderly and efficient manner, ensure adherence to management policies, safeguard the assets and secure, as far as possible, the completeness and accuracy of the records. The individual components of the control system are known as controls or internal controls.

There have been a number of listings of types of control which appear to describe universal requirements.

Figure 3.1: Internal controls

General systems controls (Auditing Practices Board)	Computer control systems (CIPFA)	Elements of a system of internal control (CIMA)
Segregation of duties	Organisational controls	Segregation of duties
Physical	Operational controls	Physical safeguards
Authorisation and approval	File and software controls	Authorisation and approval
Management	Terminal controls	Management review
Supervision	Environmental controls	Supervision
Organisation		Organisation structures
Arithmetical and accounting		Accounting
Personnel		Personnel arrangements
		Information systems
		Internal audit
		Audit committee

The APB also defined eight types of general control, listed in the table above, that apply to virtually all systems of management control. These controls are applicable to both computerised and non-computerised environments. There are various other ways to classify and describe controls. One list of controls specifically relating to computer systems was produced by CIPFA and is also shown in the table. In the final column of the table is a list of *'typical elements which together form a system of internal control'* given as Appendix 2 of CIMA's *Framework for Internal Control.*

The controls listed here are only general headings. As an example of this, operational (computer) controls listed above could be further analysed into input controls, processing controls, output controls and an audit trail.

Besides the controls themselves, the ICAEW has also suggested a number of features that usually contribute to a successful control environment. Eight of these are discussed in their *Draft Guidance for Directors of Listed Companies*, 1993, and shown in the table below.

Figure 3.2: ICAEW features for a successful control environment

Commitment to truth and fair dealing
Commitment to quality and competence
Leadership in control by example
Communication of ethical values
An appropriate organisation structure
Independence, integrity and openness at board level
Appropriate delegation of authority with accountability
A professional approach to financial reporting

3.1 Reporting on internal control

The whole internal control agenda has changed from being a system of control which would enable auditors to rely on the accuracy of records, and which would enable management to feel confident that policy was carried out and that there was no fraud, to something which must be formally reviewed and reported outside the company.

This was recognised by the CIMA *Framework for Internal Control* which explicitly discussed internal and external views of internal control, the internal view excluding internal audit and the audit committee in the sense of both being independent of executive management. The 'internal view' limited internal control to management control including internal checking.

This has been further developed by the requirement for listed companies to report on internal control under the Cadbury Code.

To comply with the Cadbury Code, listed companies must include in their annual reports for years beginning on or after 1 January 1995 a statement on internal financial control, following the Guidance issued by the Working Group in December 1994.

This must include, as a minimum:

- a statement by the directors acknowledging responsibility for the system of internal financial control;
- an explanation that this provides no guarantee – but reasonable assurance against misstatement or loss;
- a description of the key procedures that the directors have established and which are designed to provide effective internal financial control;
- confirmation that the directors (or a board committee) have *reviewed* the effectiveness of the system of internal *financial* control.

The Working Group Guidance has watered down the original Cadbury requirement that directors should report on the effectiveness of their system of internal control to a requirement to report that they have reviewed the effectiveness of the system of internal financial control.

Review only

Compliance with the Working Group Guidance by reporting that the directors have reviewed the effectiveness of the system of internal financial control does not include the need to report the results of the review. This may be surprising, but it could be argued that there is little point in publishing the vague statement of satisfaction that most would provide. Few would willingly disclose uncorrected weaknesses.

None would state that internal control was unsatisfactory.

The Guidance recommends that, where control weaknesses have given rise to material losses, contingencies or uncertainties 'which require disclosure in the financial statements or in the auditors' report' the statement should also say what corrective action has been taken or will be taken, or alternatively why no changes are considered necessary.

This presumably covers reporting after a major fraud been detected – which is too late for it to be useful.

Internal financial control

The requirement is to report on internal financial control, which is significantly narrower than internal control, excluding:

- effective and efficient operations;
- compliance with laws and regulations.

However, it is difficult to see when an organisation would report that it did not comply with laws and regulations.

Internal financial control is then defined in the Guidance as:

The internal controls established in order to provide reasonable assurance of:

(a) the safeguarding of assets against unauthorised use or disposition;

(b) the maintenance of proper accounting records and the reliability of financial information used within the business or for publication.

The Guidance encourages directors to go further, extending the scope of their statements to include the wider aspects of internal control, and giving their opinion on its effectiveness.

It is too early to form a view on how far most companies will wish to report on internal control in line with these requirements, though looking at most published accounts is encouraging in the sense of seeing considerable activity, and some variations in practice.

▪ Statements acknowledging responsibility for the system are usually formal and the wording normally follows the requirement. Occasionally there is a variation: *'The Board delegates its responsibilities for internal financial controls to strong divisional management and regional financial controllers'* (Perry Group, 1995 Report).

▪ Explanation of reasonable assurance is also usually formal, but some go further in discussing and explaining the risks. Enterprise Oil, in their statement on corporate governance, refer to the section of the financial review which deals with sensitivities and risk management, and which discusses exchange rates and crude oil prices and the use of various hedging and option techniques used to manage risks.

▪ Discussion of key procedures usually refers to budgets, performance monitoring, and the approval of investments. The level of detail provided varies considerably. Occasionally statements read differently, but reflect a clear view:

> *In view of the Company's present size, operating as a tight-knit organisation with a proven track record, in the present circumstances a number of the Cadbury proposals would not be appropriate, which is not in compliance with the Cadbury Code. Short and direct lines of communication operate between the subsidiary company managers and the main board and it has not been considered necessary to reserve a specific schedule of matters for main board consideration. The Executive continue to operate on a collegiate basis with members well equipped to provide sufficient control over the areas of responsibility of each other. In the circumstances it is felt inappropriate to set up formal Audit and Remuneration Committees or appoint three Non-Executive Directors* (Ward Holdings, 1995 Report).

▪ Statements that the directors have reviewed the effectiveness of the system of internal financial control are usually formal. Occasionally more detail is supplied:

> *Senior managers are required to sign an annual statement of compliance with key control procedures.... The system of internal control is also monitored through a programme of internal audits. The Audit Committee reviews the work of the internal audit function and approves the internal audit plan annually* (Enterprise Oil, 1995 Report).

Action required by the directors to support their reporting on internal control

This will depend on the extent of the statements that directors wish to make, or think they may need to make with further developments, and on the control environment – the inherent risk and the stage of system development. It also depends on how confident they feel about a third party, possibly their external auditors, being satisfied with the systems that exist. The actions the directors should take include:

- making arrangements for the formal consideration of internal financial control, either by placing it on the board agenda, or;
- establishing an audit committee of non-executive directors which will report back to the board, having met separately with the internal and external auditors and having considered all necessary reports;
- making arrangements to review the causes of material losses, etc., and whether they indicate a need to review systems.

Due diligence would suggest that the audit committee take many further steps:

- review of systems of authorisation and approval, the levels of authority required for various transactions, including the need for board approval for major transactions (e.g. capital expenditure) and for classes of transactions (e.g. the use of derivatives in hedging). As a minimum, such systems should be clearly documented, and all relevant instructions, which may be in internal memoranda and board minutes, consolidated and updated. There should be no room for doubt as to what the system is meant to be;
- review of the accuracy of accounting systems:
  - the comparability of management accounting and statutory accounting information
  - the reliability of forecasts and budgets
  - the extent of stock losses, and the adequacy of explanation for these;
- review of external audit reports on the financial statements, and any management letter, and a formal meeting with the auditors. If the external auditors have repeatedly drawn attention to problems, they cannot be allowed to persist;
- review of internal audit reports and formal meetings to discuss control issues and reports;
- review of the range of transactions and exposures monitored and reported internally (even if not reported externally). This applies notably to derivatives, but also to a wide range of other 'off balance sheet' transactions.

The key point is that publication is irrelevant to the need for control. Adequate control systems must exist for all transactions, and reporting systems must ensure that management, and in less detail the board, are aware of the scale of the transactions and that there are adequate control systems and regular audits.

Individual transactions that are material in size or duration, comparable with major investments, should be seen by the board in the same way.

All these transaction categories should be subject to formal risk assessment by the internal audit department and the audit committee as part of the process of agreeing the internal audit plan.

It is irrelevant to the internal auditor that there is limited external audit interest in transactions that do not have to be disclosed.

However, the aim is not to create a perfect system regardless of cost; there must be some assessment of the level of risk, which will be partly business and partly control environment.

The board should review the existence and adequacy of normal procedures such as:

▪ operating manuals;
▪ organisation structures, job descriptions;
▪ responsibility accounting, budgeting;
▪ codes of conduct, codes of ethics.

3.2 External audit and directors' reporting on Cadbury

In the same way as the board must review the effectiveness of internal financial control, but need not disclose their findings, the external auditors are required by the Stock Exchange to review certain aspects of the directors' statements, including that on internal control, but need not make public the results of this review.

The Auditing Practices Board has understandably found some difficulty with this situation, and its bulletin, *Disclosures relating to Corporate Governance*, originally issued in December 1993 (1993/2) has been revised twice: in November 1994 (1994/1), with guidance regarding the going concern concept, and in February 1995 (1995/1). The problem is in ensuring that users of financial reports do not interpret statements as implying a level of control that does not exist, or that the auditors are not in a position to assess without significant work beyond that normal in an annual audit of the financial statements. Auditors consider that they get sued often enough for matters that they agree are their responsibility, without wishing to lay themselves open to further problems.

The main difficulty for the Auditing Practices Board is the range of possible situations and statements about those situations by the directors. The main difficulty for users of accounts is that the statements that will appear in auditors' reports in due course can, at best, be described as unhelpful. To quote from the example in Bulletin 1995/1 of a proposed statement:

> *We have carried out our review in accordance with Bulletin 1995/1 'Disclosures relating to corporate governance' issued by the Auditing Practices Board. That Bulletin does not require us to perform the additional work necessary to, and we do not, express any opinion on the effectiveness of either the company's system of internal financial control or its corporate governance procedures.*

Opinion

With respect to the directors' statements on internal financial control ... in our opinion the directors have provided the disclosures required ... and such statements are not inconsistent with the information of which we are aware from our audit work on the financial statements.

The problems that have led the Auditing Practices Board to this solution have been fully discussed in its successive papers:

- *The Future Development of Auditing* (1992);
- *The Audit Agenda* (1994);
- *Internal Financial Control Effectiveness: A Discussion Paper* (April 1995).

The problems, from the external audit point of view, can be summarised as:

- the volume of work required to assess internal financial control, which involves reviewing, for instance, internal management accounts, which may not be reviewed to such a degree in a financial statement audit. There would also need to be additional work on procedures to protect the assets of the company. This work would have a significant cost, and would lead to a substantial increase in audit fees;
- the additional risk of being sued in the event of corporate disaster (though they will probably be sued in any case);
- the lack of a defining test of internal control effectiveness. It is easy to evolve a range of criteria, and of possible measures of effectiveness. It is also easy to recognise that companies face a range of business risks. But there must be some clear basis for the judgement that internal control in one company is effective, but that in another company it is not, even with apparently broadly similar systems.

There may be another way forward, with better reporting on internal financial control to shareholders coming from the audit committee of the company's board, based on the work of the internal audit department. This would prevent expensive duplication of assessment. This has been urged by both CIMA and ICAS. Unfortunately, there is still the need to formulate a defining test or tests of the effectiveness of internal control or the narrower internal financial control.

Another way forward may be taken if the government decides on legislation. It may be decided that external auditors should report on internal control. This would accord with the expectation that many users of accounts have, which is that auditors always have ensured good internal control integral to having proper books of account, and that auditors have always looked at internal control, the security of assets and the risk of fraud.

3.3 The implications of corporate governance developments for internal control

The public debate cannot be quietly closed down. It will continue, and further safeguards demanded, and eventually, in some form, provided. There will be continuing change, and it will nearly all be adding to requirements.

The days are gone when the level of required internal financial control was primarily a matter for the executive management, especially the finance director, influenced by the external auditor's management letter, and by the internal auditor function if such existed. Internal control in general was once a matter of management style, and convictions – but this era is gone. It is still best management practice, but it is now not solely management judgement.

Until recently, following the thinking behind the Auditing Practices Committee guideline, internal control was imposed by management, who were encouraged to follow the guideline as good practice, and by audit encouragement.

Internal control is now a matter which the audit committee, the non-executive directors, must assess, and report on to the shareholders. This reporting by the audit committee, or the external auditors, or both, will probably increase. The requirement now may well be to have a control system which will 'report well', i.e. which will appear to satisfy those to whom management are ultimately responsible. The level of internal control is not now primarily a management decision, though it will be considerably influenced by executive management.

This will increase the pressure on firms to have an independent internal audit function, and to increase the status, resources, and independence of the internal audit function in those firms which already have such a function. The general effect on internal systems will be:

- to increase the documentation and formality of systems, to reduce reliance on informal controls. It is easier to report on clearly defined systems, with full and up-to-date manuals;
- greater consistency between firms in board-level reporting and controls. As firms have to describe such controls, they will inevitably look at what their competitors are doing, and regard it as appropriate to control at least the same aspects of the enterprise in broadly similar ways. Firms will not wish to appear out of line with their competitors or appear to have less-effective controls;
- less risk-taking in decisions on whether controls are necessary or desirable. Judgements of the costs of additional controls versus the risks of a failure of control will be different if taken by non-executive directors, influenced by external auditors, both concerned at the risk of being sued, than if taken by executive management, considering the effect of the costs of such control systems on a bonus on profits. Neither the non-executive directors nor the auditors get a bonus on profits; their cost–benefit calculation is quite different from that of executive management;
- the particular emphasis in internal financial control as reported in published accounts on internal management accounts could well lead to these being

accorded greater importance. It could also lead to pressure for the adoption of integrated financial and management accounts because this will make it easier to report on the adequacy and accuracy of the internal accounts;

▪ the reporting in published accounts by some companies of clearly defined limits for capital expenditure authorisation, with all significant schemes requiring main board approval, could turn current good practice into virtually universal practice.

To summarise, future planning of internal control will have to recognise that interest beyond management interest is of major significance, and will continue to influence the form of control and the required level.

4 Internal Audit

A modern view of the internal audit function considers it as a function of quality assurance. As a working definition this section is about:

Ensuring that the systems in an organisation are running and producing the quality of output which is required.

This overall definition encompasses the Institute of Internal Auditors' definition of the objective of internal audit:

The objective of internal auditing is to assist members of the organisation in the effective discharge of their responsibilities. To this end internal auditing furnishes them with analyses, appraisals, recommendations, counsel and information concerning the activities reviewed.

The systems included in the quality assurance cover more than the area originally thought of as the province of the internal auditor. As examples, the operation of the following systems are specifically included:

- Transaction processing: this is the system of providing the basic information of any organisation. It refers to all kinds of processing, individually and in batches, manual and computer.
- The accounting information system: this would include the financial accounting system, the cost accounts, the management accounts and the management decision-making system.
- Production control system and other similar subsystems to the management information system.
- The system of corporate governance.

The general question to which an answer is sought is: 'How can we be assured that the company has systems that ensure it will be competently managed?'

This is a question that follows on from the basic job of a management accountant to provide information for decision-making. The discipline is intimately linked with establishing information systems and systems of management. The last few years have seen the gradual inclusion of all these areas into the internal audit function. Even if in particular entities the internal audit function has not carried out some of these activities, a number of them have been given the label 'audit'. Examples of these include systems audit, transactions audit, value-for-money audit and management (or operational) audit.

It is possible to have a quality assurance test of any system in the organisation. This section could therefore include a large number of potential audits. It briefly describes just seven of the areas typically the province of the internal audit function. Some of these are clearly central to the work of internal audit, others are often done by internal auditors as *ad hoc* (one-off) studies.

Systems audit

Figure 4.1: General audit approach

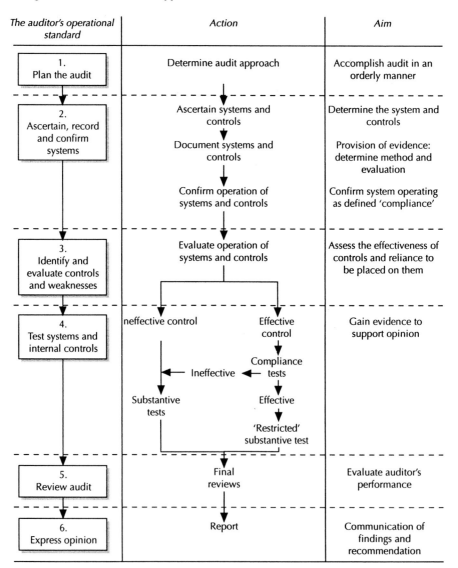

Although widely regarded as being a general systems audit, in fact this is usually restricted to the accounting system, and was initially restricted to the accounting system used to produce the annual accounts. The general idea of a systems audit is to check that the system is producing the results that would be expected. The main purpose of internal audit in this case would be to test that the internal controls are operating satisfactorily and to ensure the reliability and integrity of the data produced for management. A major task of the systems audit is to ensure that the appropriate controls are operating correctly.

The detailed methods of systems audit are discussed in later sections. These methods include three distinct ways of checking how a system works:

- checking that the system complies with the internal controls (after first having established that the internal controls are adequate for the system);
- undertaking substantive tests to check the detailed operation of the system;
- systems may also be tested using analytical review which is intended to check if the system is producing sensible results in relation to some other criteria.

In a systems audit *all three* of these would probably be used together as part of an integrated approach. Venables and Impey (1991) link these in a general audit approach which is shown in Figure 4.1.

4.1 Transactions audit

A transactions audit is defined as:

> *The vouching or proving of a large proportion of transactions to documentary evidence.* (Pratt, *Auditing*, quoted in Venables and Impey, 1991)

A transactions audit is sometimes called a *financial* or *probity* audit. It would mainly involve substantive tests and would be used where compliance tests would not be feasible, as for example in the case of an organisation with no system of internal controls. Where a systems audit is possible, a transactions audit is unlikely to be used as it is more expensive and likely to produce little more value. Internal auditors may wish to undertake a transactions audit on a new system or a pilot of a new system. A transactions audit may also be used where the cost would be significantly less than any other method, as in the case of a very small part of a business.

The transactions audit should have a limited role in internal audit, and should only be required in exceptional circumstances. In local government it is clearly regarded as part of the external audit, not the internal audit.

4.2 Value-for-money audit

Although value-for-money audit has always been called this, the technique actually involves two separate concepts:

- the concept of *calculating and evaluating* value for money for any particular activity system;
- the idea of *auditing* this value-for-money calculation.

Often, when value-for-money audit has been regarded as *audit*, it has been treated as a special investigation as if it bears no relationship to the general performance evaluation literature. It is increasingly becoming unacceptable to treat a value-for-money audit in this way as the performance evaluation literature is now expanding rapidly and encompassing much that was traditionally value-for-money *audit*.

There is still sufficient in the idea of value-for-money audits to justify this as a separate audit area within the internal audit function. The UK public sector (especially central and local government) is very much involved in post-audit of value for money.

Within the public sector, the value-for-money audit offers a useful method of checking for economy, efficiency and effectiveness in the absence of the profit measure. Value-for-money audits were introduced because market testing was regarded as impossible for most government services, and there had to be an alternative measure of efficiency. Since then, market testing and outsourcing have developed considerably, especially as the concept of the split between the functions of purchasing the service, and actually providing it, has gained wider currency. However, it has been found that services obtainable in the market may not be the same as the internal alternatives, and that there is a continuing role for value-for-money audit in balancing factors other than simple cost. The general principles of value for money are also being increasingly applied to the profit-seeking sector of the economy, especially in areas where evaluation using accounting numbers is inadequate or inappropriate.

The basic approach to value-for-money audit involves identifying and measuring four aspects of performance:

- money expended;
- inputs purchased;
- outputs achieved;
- outcomes achieved.

The relationship between money expended and inputs purchased can give a measure of *economy*. Inputs compared with outputs gives a measure of *efficiency* and outcomes compared with outputs identifies *effectiveness*.

Unfortunately, there are two severe problems with this type of analysis:

- the measurement of the items, especially outputs and outcomes for which financial and statistical measures are often unavailable;
- the appraisal of the results as the measures produced are often ratios with no absolute standards.

Over the past two decades both these issues have been widely explored. There are now many acceptable, though not perfect, measures of aspects of performance relating to specific organisations. There is also an increasing level of knowledge and agreement about what are acceptable indicators in many areas. The Audit Commission in particular has already completed a number of studies of possible measures for different areas of the public sector.

Value-for-money audits can be performed in a number of ways.

- The basic minimum is to use judgement and internal data to find internal best practice and visible waste or inefficiency, which will normally appear in the form of under-utilised staff or capital equipment – capacity to act which is not utilised. First time round, in an organisation which has not previously had an internal audit function, this can be quite effective. In the same way, a consultant working in an organisation which has had little exposure to external best practice can rapidly find some easy savings. This approach is a matter of finding obvious faults and proposing corrections.

▪ Better approaches, certainly necessary in established organisations, have to go beyond the search for obvious weaknesses. They have to involve:

  ▫ A review of the external best practice, established through interfirm comparison or benchmarking or, in the public sector, comparison of performance indicators. This will involve quite difficult judgements of the strict comparability of circumstances and data. This has been done successfully by the Audit Commission in looking at value in further education, where some colleges have quite obviously been more successful than others in getting students with limited entry qualifications through to craft qualifications.

  ▫ Some sort of engineering approach to determine what could be achieved. It is possible that all existing internal and external comparators are inefficient. An example of this is the studies done on heating costs for buildings, adjusting for varying climatic conditions in different parts of the UK, the insulation properties of the buildings, the extent to which the buildings are used, and the rapidly changing economics of using various energy sources.

  ▫ An assessment of objectives and their relationship to the cost area being studied. It is possible that, for instance, transport costs may appear high – but can be explained by policies aiming for a higher service level. This can be very difficult to assess – the key need is that, as part of the organisation, internal audit is more aware of the general issues of policy within that organisation than an external auditor or consultant would be.

It should be noted that value-for-money audit in the public sector is essentially a form of performance evaluation, invented in the public sector as a substitute for market forces, and legally required.

The Local Government Finance Act 1982 requires an external auditor to satisfy himself that 'the body whose accounts are being audited has made proper arrangements for securing economy, efficiency and effectiveness in its use of resources'.

This has, in practice, led to most authorities devoting some 30 per cent – 50 per cent of audit resources to VFM.

Generally, the auditor does not question objectives, but the extent to which they have been achieved and the means of achievement. However, it is most unlikely that there will be simple single objectives for any programme or policy. Hence, auditors are inevitably involved in issues of the clarity of objectives, the consistency of objectives, and their feasibility.

4.3 Management audit

This area of audit is about appraising the performance of managers. The CIMA *Official Terminology* defines management audit as:

> *An objective and independent appraisal of the effectiveness of managers and the corporate structure in the achievement of entity objectives and policies. Its aim is to identify existing and potential management weaknesses and to recommend ways to rectify them.*

The term *operational audit* is also used to cover this topic. The definition above suggests that management audit is extremely similar to a value-for-money audit, and clearly there are many similarities between the two areas. The chief difference is that management audit is developed mainly in relation to the commercial environment, the value-for-money audit in relation to the public-sector non-profit environment.

Management audit is a clear departure from the traditional idea that internal audit is confined to systems and transaction audits. However, management audit is clearly a part of quality assurance of systems if the system is defined as the overall management control system. In this area of audit the internal auditor works within a system of control that is less well defined than systems described above. The work is therefore subject to more subjective interpretation than the more objective systems and transactions audits.

The topics that may be covered by management audit are wide and varied. One area where this form of audit may be used is to see the extent that management is complying with management policies, for example:

- the system for approval and monitoring of capital expenditure;
- the company's car and expenses policy;
- the company's corporate code of conduct.

This is an extremely difficult area for management and for internal audit. Organisations can become very large and extend worldwide. Power is devolved to local units which are encouraged to manage within broad constraints and become entrepreneurial. If local managers are successful, senior group managers may well wish to 'turn a blind eye' to minor breaches of group rules and procedures.

The key to any successful approach is precise and consistent communication of truly important matters, and a clear statement of how breaches will be dealt with. It is futile to have frequently published threats that are never enforced.

The constant danger is that strong local teamwork leads to a strong local culture and 'local rules'. Detecting problems is difficult because local management knows that local practices can receive at best only implied consent – the issue has never come to light or been formally prohibited – and hence will not raise the issue. Local staff often perceive their loyalties to be primarily to the local unit and not to the group as a whole; they still have to work for the local managing director when the visiting group staff have returned to head office.

Management audit is clearly part of the line management control in organisations with very large numbers of establishments, whether in the UK or overseas. These establishments, especially if relatively small, may be regularly visited only by the senior manager responsible for the region and by internal audit. These have to deal with all matters arising on their visits.

Some very large organisations, such as Post Office Telephones, which became British Telecom on privatisation, used to have regional internal audit reporting to regional management, which reflected this close involvement with management. Generally such organisations have followed British Telecom in centralising internal audit as part of the process of ensuring separation and independence.

Routine audit checks may identify problems, but it is most likely that problems will come to light because:

- internal audit staff visit reasonably frequently and have gained the confidence of local staff, who hence mention problem areas in confidence;
- internal audit staff try to assess differences between local organisations, note differences in practice, and ask effective questions.

However, other areas could include:

- the company's pricing policy (especially in relation to activity costs);
- performance measurement achievements;
- the value of vehicle fleet management.

4.4 Social audit

Concern about the general accountability of companies led to the formation of the Cadbury Committee which reported in 1992. Among the recommendations of the Cadbury Committee is the general idea that companies should understand their impact on society, particularly in terms of impact on the environment, employees and in ethical areas. This is the essence of social audit.

Clearly, this again moves internal audit further still away from objective judgements towards more subjective judgements. One specific part of social audit is *environmental audit* that involves understanding and evaluating the effect of a company on its environment. Obvious areas for discussion include the impact of waste and scrap products on the environment, e.g. greenhouse gases, pollutants and energy consumption.

There are other sorts of audits, too, that organisations are being encouraged to adopt by interested parties. Examples include:

- equal opportunities audit;
- cultural audit;
- ethical audit;
- safety audit.

And many more are developing.

The common features behind these are the use of independent review, possibly by an independent expert, of activities which have previously been delegated to management and not monitored. The general approach is that there ought to be some form of control system, some sort of reporting, and that this auditing ought to be of the existence and adequacy of the control system. It is clearly a method of communicating concern and emphasising importance, and communicating values. It may be to reassure management that objectives are being achieved, or to provide assurance to a wider (stakeholder) constituency. Reference could be made by those interested in these issues to Power (1994).

4.5 Post-completion audit of capital projects

When a new project is investigated prior to its implementation, it is very likely that it will take on both a long-term and a company-wide dimension. It may also involve ethical and social issues. The success of new investment projects is crucial to the continued existence of a company, and thus monitoring and post-completion audit appraisal of these projects is essential.

Although, to some extent, detailed spending and income of projects can be monitored objectively, the fact that many projects become integrated into the general running of the company means that subjective judgement is often needed in monitoring and appraisal of these projects. Post-completion audit covers projects throughout manufacturing industry and the public sector, and from large projects to detailed small-systems implementation.

4.6 Computer auditing

Chambers, Selim and Vinten in the second edition of their book *Internal Auditing* (1990) state that *'all auditors must be computer auditors as most systems are now computerised'* (p.307). They stress the need for a high level of computer competence, possibly including a specialist.

Auditing in a computer environment is essentially the same as in a non-computerised environment in its purpose and direction but substantially different in the method of its operation. What is crucially important in computer auditing is to recognise the additional problems and controls caused by this environment. The computer environment itself is changing extremely rapidly and this change also has to be a concern of the internal auditor. The key computer auditing topics for internal audit purposes are addressed below.

Taking a brief historical perspective, the introduction first of large electro-mechanical punched-card installations, and then of mainframe installations undertaking batch processing, centralised much simple routine accounting. The early computers effectively continued with much of the routine workload of the punched-card installations, typically payroll, invoicing, sales ledgers, and simple finished stock records. This enhanced management control and simplified internal audit:

▪ processing was concentrated in one location;
▪ much more detailed procedures manuals and systems descriptions than had previously existed were required to create and operate the system. Discipline was essential in environments which could have been less organised with purely manual systems;
▪ processing was standardised – no variation was possible;

- any exceptional transactions had to be processed manually outside the basic system, which could not cope, and hence could be easily identified and reviewed;
- batch totals provided secure control on total processing.

This was further enhanced by the slow process of changing systems in any way. System change required very slow machine language programming in the absence of the more flexible and faster systems available today, and almost certainly would require redesigned input. Hence, once a system was working it was relatively simple to test what it did, and rely with minimum checks on it continuing to do the same things.

It was possible to take a 'black box' approach and work carefully around the mysterious workings which did not need to be understood (auditing round the computer). This was simplified in that the main output of early installations appeared to be listings – of inputs, of transactions, of balances, which could be checked item by item and reconciled.

These listings were the sole source of information on, for instance, the balance of stock of a particular item, and would provide the balance when the complete stock file was last updated. There was no way that only one item could be updated or even interrogated.

Hence the early computers provide no more than a highly disciplined and mechanised system of basic recording and bookkeeping.

But as computers developed into facilities which could process a much wider range of data, and process this data in different ways, it became progressively harder to justify avoiding the inner workings of the 'black box' when it could do different things. As computer systems have become more useful and are now the critical strategic resource in the management of the business, the audit and control of their operation has become progressively harder.

The audit of computer system development

The internal control and internal audit requirements fall into two broad categories, that of ensuring that the development takes place within an approved structure and under management control, and ensuring that the systems developed are suitable and controllable.

The management structure issues are easily defined and are virtually the same as those for any major investment project:

- ensure that the project is led by a senior operational manager with adequate understanding of IT;
- establish a project team representing all concerned at senior levels. This includes all users and the accounting function;
- ensure that the senior IT manager in the organisation is fully experienced, and is of an appropriate calibre, and reports at a high enough level in the organisation;
- ensure that alternative approaches have been considered;
- ensure that the project is clearly justified on financial or other grounds and

that all concerned understand the objectives of the project;

- insist that suppliers and contractors are reputable, financially sound, and that the contract is sound;
- take independent advice on the project;
- ensure that the progress of the project is monitored and reviewed by management and, if of a sufficient scale, by the board at appropriate stages;
- ensure that the project development is included in the internal audit work programme;
- consider whether the audit committee ought to include monitoring progress on the computer project in their responsibility for information systems;
- there may be circumstances in which it is appropriate for the external auditors to be asked to comment on the viability of a proposed system of strategic importance;
- make specific provision when this, like any other major project, is approved for the stages at which it will be reviewed and post-audited to ensure that the necessary data will be available.

None of these steps is guaranteed to ensure safety.

Those closely concerned with a project tend to be committed to its success, to allow enthusiasm to override managerial judgement, and fail to see warning signs. Senior managers not directly involved can recognise cost escalation and delay, but these are unfortunately normal with all large projects, whether in the IT field or elsewhere. The difficulty is recognising that the system may not work at all. The difficulties increase as systems become more fundamental to business operations, that without effective systems the business cannot operate. Examples of this are banking systems, share-dealing systems, integrated retail cash and stock management systems depending on clever tills. Once this stage is reached, computing systems are too important to be left to specialist professionals – all senior managers must have a sound understanding of the problems and potential solutions and be involved.

Reviewing the detailed implementation of the project by the systems development team is the responsibility of internal audit.

Audit of the development of systems, like the audit of investment proposals, is *pre-event auditing*, not historical auditing. Auditors are often reluctant to get involved with pre-event auditing, in case it compromises post-event audit conclusions. However, advice at this stage is much more valuable than advice after the event, when change can be inordinately expensive – and involves no more compromise than any other system recommendations.

There is sometimes a careful balance needed between demanding excessive control features in a new system, and allowing analysts to take full advantage of the flexibility of new techniques.

The objectives of a systems development audit are:

- to ensure that predetermined standards for development are satisfactory, and have been observed. This assumes that all systems development work is undertaken to an agreed protocol;
- reviewing the controls which are being built into the new system to ensure that the new system is:

- reliable and secure;
- easily auditable, or certainly feasible to audit. This does not mean perpetuating the control systems from an old computer or manual system, but ensuring that alternative controls are workable.

There should be set procedures within the organisation for the development of new systems. These should apply to all new systems, and any proposed variation should be most carefully considered.

The feasibility study should consider all alternatives before reaching a recommendation, and include a general outline of the proposed system in sufficient detail to permit sensible cost estimation.

Authorisation to proceed must come from an appropriate level within the organisation in view of the investment involved and the call on scarce staff resources.

At this stage everyone should clearly understand from the feasibility study and related proposals:

- the nature of the proposed system;
- its cost;
- the project time to completion and the times to all key intermediate stages to enable effective monitoring.

At this point the system development manager should be committed in writing to the feasibility of achieving the objectives within budget, and the user department(s) should be committed in writing to acceptance of the system as specified. If there is a problem in the user department then management or board authorisation is probably irrelevant.

At the systems design stage rules need to be established on the control of data, such issues as:

- confidentiality;
- authorisation to add data;
- authorisation to change or delete data.

It is important that there is sufficient senior user department involvement at this stage, and that it can be demonstrated by project teams and formal meetings.

The stage of program specifications and programming is that of breaking down the overall system into manageable components. At this stage the auditor needs to review:

- formal documentation;
- that the components add to the proposed whole;
- formal acceptance of specifications by project team, users and programmers. Modification after this point becomes very expensive. There should be rigorous control of proposed modifications.

Program test and approval includes not just the program, but the whole file, including:

- program specification;
- flowchart/logic diagram;

- test data;
- operating instructions.

Testing must be undertaken separately by

- programmer (and manager);
- systems development;
- users;
- internal auditors, but probably working quite closely in this with users.

Further audit work should cover

- manuals and training;
- file conversion;
- implementation, especially phased programs;
- system maintenance;
- post-audit.

Any audit of modification and maintenance work on systems has to start with the question of the audit of the original system, and the complete original system documentation, and any changes already made in the meantime.

Even assuming that all the original system was thoroughly reviewed and well documented, and meets the criteria discussed above, problems very frequently arise with systems modification. These arise because:

- modifications are made at speed, they tend to be urgent;
- documentation can be limited and completed after the modification, if at all;
- documentation tends to be separate for each modification; it does not appear necessary at the time to reformulate the total system documentation.

When the next modification proposal arises it is very difficult to see how all modifications to date fit together, and how they will be affected by the next modification.

Modern systems are much more complex than the simple systems first computerised, and it is not easy to see how all parts interrelate in detail. If this can be solved the remainder of the problem is essentially a scaled-down version of the general computer development model.

There are, however, potential safeguards in the development of computer system developments compared with the development of manual systems:

- the involvement of a range of skills. Systems development requires user specifications, systems analysis and programming. Except in the case of minor development of PC-based systems the scale is beyond one individual. Communication is required, and hence documentation normally exists. If there is documentation, audit is possible;
- the normality of outsourcing part or all the work to independent contractors. These require clear instructions as they have no prior knowledge of the organisation and its needs and customs. They also require clear instructions in self-defence – that they can say they carried out their part correctly and according to instructions even if the overall system does not do what was sought.

The combined effect of separation and frequent externalisation is to ensure in most organisations that even the most rushed modifications are documented at least in part and that audit can follow through the trail of software modification, certainly in terms of who was involved, what they attempted to do, and probably the approach taken. Following through exactly what was done, and what effects it may have had in all aspects of the overall system, depends on understanding the interrelationship of all aspects of a complex system.

There is a major problem arising from outsourcing, and from high job mobility among computer professionals; it is unlikely that those who built a new system are available in a few years to modify the system. Someone else will have to be paid to get to understand the system and then modify it.

Monitoring computer operations

Monitoring computer operations and transaction processing is much more complex now with changes away from batch processing on mainframe machines. Critical features include:

- networks; remote access, multi-user access. Some of this will be access by unauthorised or incompetent personnel, regardless of the security systems at the remote sites;
- external links; electronic data interchange (EDI), electronic payment systems, e-mail;
- databases, which have to be maintained, and which require special database management systems and clear definition of authority;
- possible real-time processing, frequently real-time data access with updating done overnight, as in some financial services institutions;
- much less documentation and listing of balances than in batch processing systems; limited documentation of inputs and outputs.

Some general principles can be suggested for the audit approach to new computer systems:

- the first priority is understanding the system and its workings, and being able to confirm that the system in use is the system documented;
- the next is to ascertain how the system can be tested. A simple approach is the use of test packs, but this is not necessarily feasible with real-time systems as the data introduced also has to be removed. It is also quite difficult to devise a test pack which tests all the features of a complex system.
  Other approaches include reviewing how system management and database management staff make their own checks on the system operation, and looking at systems of tagging predesignated transactions for subsequent evaluation;
- security needs to be reviewed, even though with scattered terminals this can be a major problem. Networks require the security of effective password control, including regular changing of passwords and control of password security, for system access and a database management system limiting access to certain parts of the data. Thus a ticket vendor can sell and reserve

seats on a particular flight, but cannot schedule an additional flight. Access to programmes, as with all systems, must be very carefully controlled. Data may have to be encrypted. Access of terminals to other computer systems needs to be controlled. Certain types of contact, e.g. EFT, must be preventable without very clear authorisation and limits;

▪ some check must be made on the accuracy of information generated by the system. If it does not correspond with reality, there must be a problem somewhere;

▪ given the lack of conventional batch totals there can be problems authorising data and transaction amendments and following these through to maintain database integrity. This is partially achieved by recording the process – possibly a data image back-up journal, keeping all amendments visible and identifiable. There must be some system of amending records to investigate;

▪ messaging of various forms is normal and processing accuracy must be investigated. It can probably best be verified at source. Message acknowledgement/confirmation systems are part of this process, but some check is required on whether these lead to any further correction. Message validity can only be verified at processing, and requires a complex structure of ensuring that only authorised categories of transactions for authorisable amounts are actioned – an audit trail to find out later what has gone wrong is not sufficient;

▪ data validity checking needs reviewing. Most validity tests are reasonableness tests – size of transaction, existence of all relevant data, valid codes.

Quite sophisticated approaches are being developed, for instance by credit card companies, to identify from historical patterns normal and abnormal transactions. Similar monitoring systems, based on cusum techniques, can identify normal and abnormal patterns of terminal usage.

Batch accuracy cannot be checked, but transactions must be recorded on at least a daily basis, probably a shift basis, by terminal. This will enable errors to be found. However, the transactions will have taken place and it may not be possible to 'back out' errors or batches of transactions containing errors;

▪ Back-up of some form is the first step towards system security and preventing disasters. Back-up may well be in the form of an overnight back-up, and a log of the day's transaction. This, in principle, can enable data to be recreated, but this assumes that facilities are available for such exercises, which can be problematical given the size of the systems involved;

▪ Recovery procedures will need to cover central processor, terminal and line failure, and systems will need to be able to deal with messages in transit.

To summarise, the approach needed is to look for new ways to make tests which perform the same purpose of assessing the system and its inherent problems. There is no merit in insisting on the same tests as before if newer ones achieve the same results.

Testing should include the use of CAATs (computer-assisted audit techniques):

- database interrogation. This would usually be through the database management facilities, rather than using specially created programs, to avoid complications.

  Generalised audit enquiry software is not likely to be as effective, and would need extensive testing before being used on the system – but may enable different, more relevant, questions to be asked;
- analysis of trends, account details.

  Reasonableness tests as validity tests will include much trend analysis; there is no merit in duplicating this.

  Using portable PCs enables a more sophisticated analytical review:
  □ regression analysis
  □ using financial data available on CD and creating appropriate interfirm comparisons using such products as Lotus;
- program code comparison programs to verify program changes;
- logic path analysis programs to convert to structure diagrams/flowcharts for audit analysis:
  □ these together should enable the auditor to confirm that the system is doing what it was intended to do, if properly used;
- integrated audit monitors may be built into the system, which may tag accounts and/or transactions, or record data for subsequent analysis. Audit may have to depend quite heavily on these systems. This could be the most practical way of following a transaction through the system.

Computer security and disaster planning

This is essential. There are enough disasters to necessitate logical planning to minimise the effects.

However, maintaining an ideal back-up system is very expensive and realistic assessment is needed of the consequence of failure, and the action taken in the event of failure.

Planning falls into two categories:

- ensuring that duplicate data is kept securely and separately from the main installation, and is continually updated. This is the absolute minimum. Businesses tend to fail if they lose all their data;
- ensuring that there are processing back-ups commensurate with the problem and potential loss. This calculation will look very different in, for instance, the following circumstances:
  □ mission-critical military applications;
  □ airline ticket sales;
  □ retail supermarket sales when the tills fail through a power failure;
  □ inability to process payments to suppliers for a month.

New developments in computing

There are always new and exciting developments being announced in computers, and many of them work.

The benefits are always seen early by enthusiasts, and there may be significant commercial advantages in being 'ahead of the game'.

The key internal control and internal audit problems are:

- there is no such thing as a system without problems, and trying to analyse a new system to see what the problems might be, before it has been tested in depth in a live application, is extremely difficult;
- if there is uncertainty regarding the problems, there will be greater uncertainty regarding the controls needed, as opposed to the printouts and reports that 'might be useful';
- approaches may have to be taken of estimating the risks involved and taking calculated chances.

There will always be new developments, and new control problems, and internal auditors will have to accept that at no point will it be possible to say that a system is fully developed and tested and will not need any further change.

4.7 Organisation of the internal audit function

As with any other service in organisations, there is no ideal or single solution to the question of organisation of this department. There are a number of important issues to consider in this decision, and this section will outline these.

The internal auditor has tasks that are outlined in the previous section. From the objectives it is possible to determine a number of important aspects of the internal auditor's position within an organisation. These include:

- independence from influence by those being investigated; freedom from bias, and an ethical approach. Independence includes commanding resources to undertake the tasks set;
- expertise, increasingly in a wide variety of disciplines including accounting;
- authority in order to access areas which may need investigating but which are sensitive.

We shall now look at each of these in turn.

Independence

The Auditing Practices Board has stated that:

> *The internal auditor should have the independence in terms of organisational status and personal objectivity which permits the proper performance of his duties.*

If the internal auditor is to have this sort of independence, he/she must have sufficient freedom not to be influenced by other members of the organisation. The organisation could influence an internal auditor by being able to:

- control the resources of the internal audit department;
- block the reports of the internal auditor to higher levels of management;
- insist that work is carried on in a particular fashion or at a particular time;
- insist that the internal auditor assists with other management or accounting duties.

Independence must mean the avoidance of all these things. A starting-point for this is ensuring that the function is answerable to only the highest level of management. This could be the board of directors, though even answerability at this level means that the internal auditor is precluded from investigating board-level decisions without the prior consent of the board. The solution that currently seems to find most favour is to have the internal auditor answerable to an audit committee of the board. The non-executive directors of the board would be the main members of this committee. The level of resourcing, tasks to be undertaken and reporting thus becomes a responsibility of the very highest level of management.

Where such direct appointment by the board or its audit committee is not possible, the internal auditor must still ensure that independence of the department is emphasised at every opportunity. Besides the ability to be answerable to top management, other factors which are necessary for independence include:

- it must have the support of management at all levels;
- priorities must be established within the internal audit function, subject only to the general programme agreed by the audit committee;
- internal auditors must be free from personal bias, for example friendships with other members of the management team;
- the internal audit staff should also be free from undue influences within the company.

A second aspect of the internal auditor's independence is his or her professional standing together with the ethical code of conduct with which he is charged. Although much of the work which the internal auditor does is likely to be subjective, sufficient guidelines exist within the internal audit profession to ensure that such subjective views are validly taken.

Although independence of internal auditors is necessary for the completion of the work they do, it can create behavioural conflicts within the organisation. One such conflict is when the internal auditor gives advice on the development of a computer system that he/she will subsequently be involved in monitoring.

Despite being independent, internal auditors work for the benefit of the company. Thus their work can contribute to the objectives of the organisation. However, internal auditors can also be viewed, within an organisation, as 'police' whose sole job is to be critical and unhelpful. If moves are made by internal audit to take on a more friendly stance this can be extremely good for the organisation but may destroy the independence of the internal auditor. The internal auditor therefore treads a very fine line between usefulness to the organisation and independence from it.

The problem of independence also affects the problem of career progression for members employed by the internal audit department. If staff are freely interchanged between internal audit and operating departments, then the chance of independence being compromised is increased many times. This latter problem may be less severe in very large companies where internal auditors may be confined to certain divisions. In large companies, one possible answer to this problem is for internal audit to be the first entry point for staff from public practice, who then move on to normal accounting. Although, on independence grounds, there is rarely a case for moving an accountant from a normal accounting job to internal audit, some companies use internal audit as part of career development of staff.

The issue of preserving independence is a major determinant of any assessment of the internal audit function.

The Standards for the Professional Practice of Internal Auditing (IIA) require an external review of internal audit departments at least once every three years. However, less than half of the private-sector organisations comply with this.

The possible choices for the review include:

- review by another internal auditing department. This is possible and easy to arrange within a very large group where there may be different departments in different parts of the group, though whether this would be truly independent is doubtful;
- peer review by internal auditors from other firms. Here the reviewers would be most qualified and competent, but there could be considerable problems with issues of the confidentiality of information, and management may regard the review as likely to lead to professionals protecting each other;
- review by the external auditor. The danger here is that the external auditor will tend to review the work in terms of the criteria that they themselves use to assess the extent to which they can rely on internal audit in the course of the external audit. It is important to assess internal audit against the agreed policies and programme;
- review by consultants. This would depend on the skill and experience of the consultants. Unless they have relevant experience it could be very expensive for the benefit obtainable;
- review by a non-executive director. If a non-executive director has a financial background and the time and willingness to carry out the review, this could be the best approach.

A review of internal audit could lead to recommendations to spend more (or less) on the function, to change the management of the function, to contract out the function. Post-Cadbury, it cannot easily recommend the total abolition of the function.

It is probably sensible to be realistic about how much can be done by levels of reporting and the establishment of an audit committee to ensure independence within an organisation. The key to the organisational arrangements is not their formal structure, but the acceptance by senior operational management in the organisation that internal audit should be independent and should be respected. If such managers regard the function as a time-wasting nuisance, it is not likely to be successful.

Authority

The discussion above on independence suggests that an auditor needs a certain amount of distance from the organisation. However, in order to perform any sort of work within the organisation the internal auditor needs authority. Weber (1947) suggested that there are three pure types of legitimate authority:

- rational grounds, i.e. legal authority;
- traditional grounds, i.e. traditional authority;
- charismatic grounds, i.e. charismatic authority.

This early view of authority can be found repeated in more recent books and is extremely helpful in understanding the authority needed by the internal auditor. Peabody (1962) expanded these three levels of authority into four:

- authority of legitimacy;
- authority of position;
- authority of competence;
- authority of person.

In terms of the internal auditor, each of these types of authority is needed in the work that is required.

Legitimacy is required in order to gain access to documents and personnel within an organisation. While external auditors may gain their legitimacy through Acts of Parliament, the internal auditor is much more likely to gain his/her authority by virtue of the delegation of the task from the board or central management.

The internal auditor does not have legal powers beyond those of the company or a normal individual. This is a very important distinction when it comes to discussing the extent of the investigative powers of internal auditors.

This 'legal' authority would probably give the internal auditor power to access company documents, even those regarded as confidential, and to ask employees legitimate questions about their work as employees and in relation to company matters. Sometimes the board may limit the power of internal auditors, especially for particular investigations, though the board may also be prepared to extend additional powers for certain investigations.

Alongside the actual legal authority given to the internal auditor a grant of sufficient resources is needed to execute the legal authority. It is pointless having the authority to demand sight of documents in a distant subsidiary, if this authority does not come with the ability to travel to that subsidiary or to demand transmission of those documents to the auditor.

Authority of position is important to the internal auditor, chiefly because of the auditor's position independent from the rest of the organisation. However, internal auditors themselves have their own hierarchy and the chief internal auditor will carry a much more positional authority to obtain information than a junior clerk in the department. Such authority needs to be carefully weighed against the benefits. It may thus be appropriate for members of the internal audit department, with little authority, to deal with transactional and straightforward compliance work, but it would be inappropriate for them to be used in more complex or sensitive situations where higher-position authority would carry more weight with those being investigated. This particular type of authority is of less importance in an internal audit department than in other areas because most internal audit departments are relatively small and, in any case, have significant authority because of their 'legal' position. This general situation is similar to the police force where most routine work does not demand the intervention of someone of higher rank than a normal officer.

Competence authority is something that the internal auditor requires in order to be taken seriously both by senior management and by the rest of the organisation. The internal auditor must be at least as competent as the staff who are being investigated or controlled. Although this can be a *Catch 22* situation when internal auditors need to be trained, this professional legitimacy is vital if the internal auditor is going to be giving advice or discussing how to solve problems.

The traditional professional competence of internal auditors is in the area of accounting. However, there is a demand for wider ability as multidisciplinary studies are necessary, especially for value-for-money audit. The wider breadth of skills for internal auditors include:

- computer auditing skills, possibly extending as far as programming;
- knowledge of personnel management issues, industrial relations and psychology;
- production and marketing management and quality control skills.

There is an interesting question about what an internal audit team should do when the necessary expertise for an investigation does not exist within the group. There are two ways to gain this expertise: specific training of one or more members of the team; or the buying in, either short or long term, of necessary help. Which approach should be taken will depend on long-term cost-benefit situations. Increasingly, however, internal auditors need to train in more fields than accounting, auditing and tax. Training may have to be 'off the job' in order not to conflict with independence.

Charismatic authority is the most difficult type of authority to train for and yet it is the most important authority needed for certain types of internal audit work. If the internal auditor is seen as a policeman then such charismatic authority, though useful, is not vital. If, however, the internal auditor takes on roles as adviser then the more formal legal authority can actually hinder the work. Chambers (1991) shows how the contrast between formal (legal, etc.) and informal (charismatic) authority matches different roles.

Figure 4.2: Conflicting roles for the internal auditor

Role/task	Policeman	Adviser
Authority	Formal	Informal
Source of authority	Office	Personal abilities
Sanction	Coercion	Suggestion

Adapted from Chambers (1991)

Charismatic authority needs to be developed by internal auditors who must be able to have good communication skills and be able to relate easily to the people in the organisation with whom they are dealing.

Role conflict

It is evident from this discussion that the internal auditor may face a conflict of roles. This is inevitable in view of the wide range of tasks that are required of an internal auditor. The level of conflict is likely to increase as the range of jobs taken on by the internal audit department increases. It is one of the new challenges for internal auditors to be able to meet this role conflict head on.

This is heightened by the increased expectations in the post-Cadbury environment. Relatively few years ago internal audit could be justified as providing an independent assessment of control which helped management ensure a sound control environment, and this could be justified as helping long-term profitability. In the new environment, there are raised expectations that the same function, possibly with increased resources and status, can provide the non-executive directors, and through them the shareholders, reasonable assurance concerning internal control.

It is possible that internal audit, to meet increased expectations, will require much-enhanced staff skills and status and a new internal audit management approach. Many organisations are 'buying in' such skills, especially specialist skills, by outsourcing the provision of internal audit services, often to major audit firms.

Authority limits

It is important to realise that there are areas where the internal auditor has no authority. One of the main sources of the legal authority that the internal auditor has is that he/she is able to report findings to the board. In the same way that the policeman has no authority to extract punishment from an offender or to demand that a particular risk situation is corrected, so the internal auditor has no authority to institute change in any areas subject to audit nor to punish any offender who might be discovered in the course of the investigation. This limitation on power is in itself an area of authority in that it enhances the professional standing of the internal auditor to one of investigator and adviser rather than instigator and punisher. Any action that the internal auditor may take should not extend to correcting mistakes, merely to investigating and reporting them.

Relationships with the external auditor

The internal and external auditors essentially have two different roles: the internal to serve management's control function needs, the external to establish that the accounts provide a 'true and fair view' of the company's performance and position. However, there is an overlap of duties, training, methodology and expertise between the two functions and there is some similarity in status between them. Two areas of relationship are discussed here: external reliance on internal work done and the use of external audit for internal audit work.

External reliance on internal work done

The Auditing Practices Board recognises that the work done by internal audit may be relied upon by the external auditor. Statement of Auditing Standards 500, *Considering the Work of Internal Audit*, in paragraphs 6 and 7, states:

> *The role of internal audit is determined by management and the directors and its objectives differ from those of the external auditors, who are engaged to report independently on the financial statements. The external auditor's primary concern is whether the financial statements are free of material misstatement. The internal audit function's objectives vary according to the requirements of management and the directors and, generally, less emphasis is placed on materiality considerations.*
>
> *Nevertheless, some of the means of achieving their respective objectives are often similar and thus certain of the work of internal auditors may be useful in determining the nature, timing and extent of external audit procedures. If an entity has an audit committee, monitoring the activities of the internal audit function and the relationship between the entity's internal and external auditors is often one of that committee's responsibilities.*

If this can be relied on, the external auditor's workload may be substantially reduced. This will produce benefits to the company if the internal auditor checks on agreed aspects as part of the normal workload. However, to allow the external auditor to rely on the internal auditor's work, several factors are regarded as essential:

- there must be a high level of independence of the internal auditor;
- the terms of reference of the internal audit in respect of the tasks to be relied on must be relevant to external audit;
- the internal audit work must be executed in a professional manner, especially in terms of planning, control, review and working papers;
- the staff must be technically competent and adequately trained;
- the internal audit department must be adequately resourced;
- the reports prepared should be of adequate quality and be taken seriously by management.

Obviously it is the responsibility of external auditors to satisfy themselves as to the adequacy of the internal audit department's work. Management could well see this assessment as a quality indicator of its internal audit department, though failure to meet the criteria may be due to matters beyond the control of the internal audit department (e.g. independence).

Post-Cadbury, the prime responsibility for reporting to shareholders on internal control is that of the directors; external audit reporting is extremely limited. If the requirement for reporting on internal control by external auditors is extended, and it could well be in due course, as there is a considerable 'expectations gap' between the audit report and the normal shareholder expectation, this could transform the relationship between internal and external audit.

Use of external audit for internal audit work

There are occasions where it may be sensible to use external auditors to do work normally done by internal auditors. It may be cheaper (as for instance for an overseas subsidiary), they may have specialist staff and services that are not available internally or it may be ethically more correct to use a completely independent investigator. If external auditors are used then they will need to ensure that performing the investigation necessary will not jeopardise their independence or produce a conflict of interests in relation to their main task. In an internal audit role they will be working primarily for management and not for the shareholders. Often, of course, the two roles coincide.

4.8 Quality assurance in internal audit

In this section some of the general ways in which internal auditors proceed with investigations are briefly discussed. The first section introduces a general approach to internal audit work and the following sections give details of how certain types of investigations are carried out. In each of these types of investigation there are common methods that may be used and the more important of these are detailed later.

A general approach to internal audit work

Internal auditing should take a careful, rigorous approach to investigating issues. Whatever the issue to be investigated, the following general actions would be part of the approach.

- Identify objectives for the investigation: this might involve seeking clarification of the terms of reference and having these clearly stated. There may be multiple objectives.
- Identify the subject-matter to be investigated: this may be the systems in operation or individuals or parts of the organisation.
- Examine the problem in relation to the subject-matter and draw up a plan of action to investigate the problem. Drawing up measurement criteria, preparing risk profiles and establishing relevant standards may be a part of this step. This stage (and the next) may need to be repeated after initial data-gathering.
- Allocate resources and staff to the problem.
- Gather information about the subject-matter as appropriate. This may involve using a variety of data-gathering and recording techniques.
- Assess the data gathered in relation to the investigation problem. This may mean, for instance, testing a system against an internal control questionnaire or assessing value-for-money measures against standards.

- Reach a conclusion and, if appropriate, check this against the initial problem.
- Identify any actions necessary as a result of the investigation.
- Check for completeness and review the work done by subordinates.
- Report to management.

Inevitably, not all investigations will proceed in this order. In particular, adverse findings in part of the investigation (such as a control system not working properly) may mean a repeat of earlier stages. However, these are the elements that ought to be present and it ought to be possible to introduce a control system that checks that stages are completed.

Analytical review

Definition and introduction

The CIMA *Official Terminology* defines analytical review as:

> *The examination of ratios, trends and changes in balances from one period to the next, to obtain a broad understanding of the financial position and results of operations; and to identify any items requiring further investigation.*

Analytical review is mainly used in external audit work where it is important for auditors to express an opinion on the accounts. However, the use of analytical review techniques can be extremely helpful in coming to an understanding of problems within the company. Two important points need to be made about analytical review in today's manufacturing environment.

- Analytical review may be performed differently in different organisations because of their different industry, area of operations, management style and objectives. It is therefore not adequate to simply learn a long list of techniques and list these for every situation. Instead, it should be appreciated how various techniques apply to appropriate situations.
- The traditional analytical review techniques of ratios, budget/actual comparison and of balance comparison need to incorporate both *financial measures* and increasingly *non-financial measures* of quality output and outcomes.

Figures used for analytical review can indicate whether an operation is efficient or not, but only if the figures used are correct. If there are unusual fluctuations this may indicate that there are material errors and/or fraud. This is one of the uses of analytical review by external auditors and it can be equally useful to internal auditors.

The starting-point of much analytical review is the use of ratio analysis. Ratios are required for two main purposes: to normalise and to measure efficiency and effectiveness. Normalisation removes the effect of size from accounts. The normalisation function is particularly important where ratios are to be compared across companies or divisions. It is thus possible, for example, to produce a profit and loss account where every item is expressed as a percentage of sales or a balance sheet where each item is expressed as a percentage of capital employed.

This may also be useful to compare year on year or across different-sized divisions and companies.

Ratio analysis is extremely important in internal audit to identify efficiency and effectiveness. These concepts measure output (or outcomes) in relation to inputs (or outputs) and thus the measures themselves are ratios. There are two ratio pyramids, one which links the *financing* ratios and is mainly the concern of the finance discipline and another which consists of all the *operating* ratios.

The standard financial ratios depend mainly on the use of financial information. As more quality issues are considered, management accountants and internal auditors must be increasingly prepared to introduce and explore other ratios which will be valuable in specific circumstances. Figure 4.3 lists some of the ratios highlighted in Niall Lothian's book *Measuring Corporate Performance* (1987).

The public sector computes a multitude of performance indicators that can be used in an analytical review.

Figure 4.3: Ratios

Name	*Calculation*
Machine efficiency	$\dfrac{\text{Actual hours available}}{\text{Target hours available}}$
Asset productivity	$\dfrac{\text{Monthly production costs (inc. bought-in parts)}}{\text{Inventory plus manufacturing plant plus space costs}}$
Linearity of productivity	$\dfrac{\text{Actual production from beginning to end}}{\text{Planned production from beginning to end}}$
Productivity	$\dfrac{\text{Volume of throughput}}{\text{Gross hours}}$
Overtime production	$\dfrac{\text{Overtime}}{\text{Gross hours}}$
Arrears of products shipped	$\dfrac{\text{Unshipped orders which missed the contracting date}}{\text{Annual production}} \times 52$
Inspection failure rates	$\dfrac{\text{Actual failure rate}}{\text{Target failure rate}}$

How analytical review is practised

Analytical review ought to be done scientifically. The purpose of the review is to obtain an understanding of what has happened and to identify unusual situations. The auditor should adopt a scientific hypothesis testing approach to the review. In its simplest form, hypothesis testing involves:

■ Producing a single well-defined question in the form of a statement such as 'if the process is proceeding correctly, the results should be within 2 per cent of the budget'. This identifies a particular aspect to be investigated.

■ Producing the data to test the hypothesis. This may include both actual data and a standard against which that is going to tested. The test may be taken against a budget, previous years' figures, other organisations' figures, or, if none of these exist, some predefined appropriate standard such as an industry average or an auditor's prior experience.

■ Once the data has been obtained, the actual figures will be compared with the standard.

■ A measure of the difference and its significance needs to be established between the standard and the actual and any deviation which exceeds this standard will need to be investigated further.

■ A conclusion is then drawn about the original question.

There are, of course, few analytical review situations where only a single question (or hypothesis) would be posed. This approach is fairly standard in auditing generally. Analytical review is dependent on having some standard against which to compare. Where this is not available, as in the case of new measures, efforts will be needed to produce such standards. Particular problems exist within the public sector in relation to new performance measurements and a number of bodies including the Audit Commission and CIPFA have attempted to provide such measurements and standards in new areas.

In the review of various accounting ratios there is a great danger in believing that there is a 'good' ratio which is universally applicable. Different industries and trading environments are likely to give rise to different ratios. Interpretation therefore has to be taken with a great deal of care even though there would be some ratios which would be widely regarded as being extremely serious for any company.

It is important not to take the limited view of analytical review often taken by external audit. Internal audit has access to the full range of internal management information, sales, production, quality statistics, and management accounting information.

Where an organisation operates through a large number of local branches, such as branch banks, or large retail operations, the process of analysing and comparing branch operations is crucial to operational management. Hence management will already have reviewed the figures that the internal auditor is using for analytical review and it may well be helpful to discuss their findings and perceptions of the problem areas. Some variations of the figures from the expected can have easy explanation in operational problems which managers are aware of but auditors may not realise exist. Other variations interest internal audit more than they initially interested management.

Goal analysis

Goal analysis is really an extension of analytical review into the area of discovering the goals of the organisation and the extent to which those goals have been met. Effectively, therefore, goal analysis moves the internal auditor into the area of strategic planning compared with the more regular analytical review which looks at operational and management time-scales. Goal analysis may of course not just be related to the strategic level, but this is the level at which it seems to be of most importance. One area where goal analysis is extremely useful is in the area of value-for-money audit, particularly in the public sector.

Goal analysis is most useful when objectives are unclear or there are multiple objectives.

Post-completion auditing

Post-completion auditing (post-audit) of investment projects is now firmly recommended as a part of the capital budgeting process. Post-auditing is considered as a key example of an internal audit procedure: the technical details are discussed only briefly. The purpose of post-auditing is to examine how well or badly a project has performed after (i.e. post) it has been implemented. Post-audit may be undertaken at any stage after a project has been started and need not wait until after the project has been completed – despite the title to this section. Neale (1991) suggests that there are at least seven distinct benefits from post-auditing. These are:

- Improved quality of decision-making: this is a feedback mechanism from the audit suggesting changes that need to be made to the process of decision-making.
- Improved realism of project appraisals: this is to attempt to prevent biasing upwards of cash flow in proposals.
- Improved corporate performance: brought about by not choosing projects with low yields.
- Identification of key variables: this after-the-event (*ex post*) knowledge can help to identify what the actual key variables were compared with the ones that were thought to be the case before implementation (*ex ante*).
- Improved internal control mechanisms: this is brought about simply by the presence of post-audit; however, in view of the infrequency of post-audits, the benefit of this may be negligible.
- More frequent project termination: although firms are often unwilling to stop unsuccessful projects, it may be the logical thing to do. Performing post-audit actually gives the information to make that decision.
- Enables rapid adjustment to under-performing projects: this, of course, is a prime feedback function of post-audit.

Issues relating to post-completion audit

Post-audits can be one-off investigations as and when necessary, or they can be set up as a formal permanent internal audit function. The approach taken will depend on the size of the firm, the number of capital projects undertaken, and the general view of management as to the importance of post-audit in their decision-making. One-off post-audits are likely to be more expensive per unit than more regular post-audits, but there may be strong justification for the one-off approach.

Whether post-audit is one-off or regular, a number of key implementation issues are necessary. These are listed and briefly described below, though the various factors may be more or less important to particular organisations.

Projects to audit

Although all projects ought to be available for post-audit, there is a decreasing marginal value as more projects are analysed. The choice of projects must therefore be a cost-benefit decision. This must consider the purpose of post-audit and the risk of not doing post-audit in particular projects. Among the factors which suggest that no post-audit is needed are:

- the small size of the project;
- the project is unlikely to be repeated;
- the project has mechanisms of control that are strong, e.g. newly established subsidiary;
- a project where other factors have already led to abandonment.

The opposite of these factors – large size, many similar projects, large value or projects which would otherwise not be considered for abandonment – all indicate that post-audit should be undertaken.

It is important to establish the risk factors and general policy of selecting projects for post-audit in advance. This avoids the charge of bias in selecting for audit projects of particular divisions or particular managers. Where necessary, random selection can be undertaken and it may be appropriate to use some form of selective sampling, e.g. more larger than smaller projects. Whatever method is chosen, the cost of doing the audit must be considered seriously in relation to the total benefit that might be gained.

Point at which project is audited

A further issue connected with the choice of project is the decision at what point or points within a project's life to make the audit. Audit too early in a project's life may produce an incorrect result because of timing differences in cash flows. Though timings will have been suggested in a project proposal, changes may happen that look significant but that are well within the bounds of viability for the project. Similarly, too late an audit may mean that the project cannot be corrected or abandoned without significant losses to the firm. It is not possible to set a definitive rule for when post-audit should take place: anything from one year to five years or more may be acceptable. One possible solution to this problem is to ask each project proposer to nominate the points at which post-audit should be undertaken for their project.

Who will complete post-audit?

This is a particular problem with the one-off audit, though it may be a problem with more regular audits when projects are of diverse character. Each different type of project will need different expertise in the appraisal: perhaps engineering skill in production and development, marketing and development in a new product launch, etc. Where such diversity does not exist it may be that the internal audit team would have sufficient ability to deal with most post-audits. However, where diversity is present, then a post-audit committee may be formed with people co-opted from areas of particular expertise. A great deal of care needs to be taken with the choice of post-audit team, particularly where inter-divisional rivalry may be involved.

The techniques used in post-audit need to be clearly decided before an investigation takes place. Probably the best time to decide is at the project appraisal stage prior to its implementation. Post-audit should cover two areas: monitoring and appraisal. Monitoring would be the gathering of information for appraisal and appraisal would be formal judgement of how a project is performing in relation to predetermined guidelines. The quality of the final appraisal can be considerably enhanced if the original project proposal has clearly spelt out both financial and non-financial objectives for the project. The actual techniques used for appraisal will vary from project to project, but should include some comparative analysis with, for example, previous periods, previous projects, other divisions, other industries.

Post-audit will not just consider the outcome of a particular project, but also the process by which the project has been approved and implemented. This may itself be compared with standard procedures of the firm and the original timetable set for the project.

A theme which is recurrent throughout these previous paragraphs is that post-audit is considerably simplified if the possibility of it is considered at the project application stage. If the application considers appraisal, then monitoring needed for the appraisal can be set up from the very start of the project. Therefore one of the success factors of the post-audit is almost certainly the existence of post-audit itself.

Problems of post-completion audit

Though the prevalence of post-audit is increasing within the economy, it is clear that there are many problems associated with its use. This section summarises a few of these though individual organisations may encounter specific problems of their own.

Separating variables and data for the project
Few projects in a large company are intended to stand alone. As a result, while it might be possible to identify start-up costs associated with the project, it may be extremely difficult to identify recurrent costs, benefits and problems which relate to the project alone. There may be a particular problem, for example in investigating the success of one new machine that is one of many in an integrated factory. This lack of data could be an additional reason for not undertaking a particular audit. However, it is not itself a sufficient reason to prevent a post-audit. Other data (even if less objective) may be available and there may be valuable lessons to be learnt from the implementation. If separate and identifiable data is not available then great care needs to be taken with the interpretation of results. This is particularly the case where apportionment of costs is needed.

Dealing with changing conditions

In an unstable world, environmental conditions envisaged in project proposals rarely occur in practice. Thus the results of a project may be different mainly because of the changed conditions. Although this may limit the ability to appraise the project, there are still valuable lessons that may be learned from the prediction mechanisms and the ability of the project implementation to adapt to changed environments.

Potential for adverse effects of post-audit

The behavioural implications of monitoring are well known in other areas. The introduction of monitoring and evaluation in post-audits will have similar effects: some of these will relate to the proposal stage where, for example, risky but profitable projects may not be undertaken. Behavioural impacts may also be found in the actual audit itself where attempts may be made to hide potentially embarrassing problems, even when an understanding of these could assist the firm in the development of future projects. Behavioural considerations lead to a number of important areas for debate, especially the extent to which top management should support post-audit.

The format of the original project proposal

The original project may have been designed in such a way that it is not amenable to audit because of either its structure or outcomes. For example, the original appraisal technique may include outcomes that are impossible to measure. In order to overcome this problem projects should be designed with a specific aim of being audited.

Accessibility to information

Post-audit needs to be able to get access to the relevant data for audit. However, if some of this data is external to the organisation or it is excessively subjective or confidential, then it may be extremely difficult to produce a reasonable post-audit study.

Implementation of post-completion audit

In outline the procedure for implementing any individual post-audit will be similar to any other one-off quality assurance procedure. In broad outline terms this will consist of the following steps:

- set objective;
- appoint team;
- collect monitoring data;
- evaluate monitoring data;
- draft report and discuss with management;
- prepare full recommendations and report;
- report to top management;
- top management implement action recommended.

Adaptation of this general framework to particular circumstances will take account of variations in project size, length, complexity and difficulty.

Fraud: with special reference to computer fraud

Why computers make fraud easier

Fraud takes place in both computerised and non-computerised environments. However, computer environments have properties making fraud easier to undertake and more difficult to detect. These situations relate to the following key areas.

Centralisation

This is a particular problem as three specific areas are centralised:

(a) Data (particularly with databases): accessibility becomes easier and thus the dangers of loss and manipulation become greater;
(b) Functions: the basic control of segregation of duties is lost;
(c) Operations: this is in order to make the best use of technology but it again makes for easier manipulation by a perpetrator of fraud.

Difficulty of physical controls

Computer records are not visible and therefore it is difficult to trace records and ensure an audit trail. The lack of visibility is such that both programs and data can be altered without trace. It is important for those without computer experience to realise how easy this is. Utility programs allow direct access to data on disk and allow alteration of individual bytes without leaving any record. In addition, data can be deliberately removed from files without trace and files can easily be copied without trace. Gradual improvements in encryption of data are making certain aspects of this more difficult but encryption is not yet widely used in business computer files.

The introduction of microcomputers is causing additional problems for the detection of fraud. In particular, controls found in the mainframe environment are more difficult to implement on smaller operating systems. Networked microcomputer systems can be made relatively secure but still lack many of the standard mainframe controls. Though fraudulent actions in these areas are likely to be committed by experts, many people have the expertise, especially as more computers become networked microcomputers.

Complexity

It is difficult to understand how programs work, even for the expert. As programs become more sophisticated and there is increased use of packages, where the source code is not available, it becomes more difficult to understand exactly what a computer is actually doing. In addition, technical personnel can often circumvent controls.

Control v. efficiency

This is a particular problem with on-line systems and microcomputers but will also apply to mainframe applications. Increased control reduces efficiency (i.e. costs money) and makes the computer slow down for the user. In addition, systems design for control is expensive. As a result control may be poor in areas that need to be run efficiently. One of the key areas where control is poor is with spreadsheets where the need for rapid calculation means that control is likely to be poor. However, spreadsheets often deal with calculations peripheral to the main data store of organisations.

The prerequisites for fraud and their prevention

There are three prerequisites for fraud to occur: dishonesty, opportunity and motive. The omission of any one should stop the fraud. The honest person is unlikely to commit fraud even given the opportunity and the motive. As a result of this it is possible to specify a group of controls to prevent each of these occurring and these are shown below:

To deal with:	Prevention of fraud needs:
Dishonesty	Careful scrutiny of staff: supervision and interest in their lifestyle;
	Severe discipline for offenders;
	Screening of new employees on appointment (references, bonding, possibly personality checks);
	Moral leadership by managers and board members.
Opportunity	Separation of duties, however difficult this might be to achieve;
	Input and output controls on computer processing;
	Control and testing of program changes;
	Physical security of hardware and assets;
	Internal controls (e.g. passwords);
	Control over issue of output forms (especially cheques).
Motive	Good employment conditions;
	Instant dismissals where necessary;
	Sympathetic complaints procedure.

These controls are mainly standard internal controls, though there are some additional ones in the area of personnel management and morality that may be unfamiliar (and possibly unpopular). In addition to the above controls, it is important to have a working detection system comprising (at least):

- An audit trail;
- Logging of access, particularly to remote terminals, sensitive files, operating system, tape library and utility programs;
- Good documentation of all programs;
- Restricted use of and logging of compiler use.

Uncovering fraud

Discovering fraud is exceptionally difficult, and perhaps the majority of frauds both with and without computers are found by accident. Well-operated controls should prevent fraud taking place but, as one of the ways fraud is committed is to circumvent controls, these may be inadequate to discover it is occurring. There are some key ways of uncovering fraud:

- Perform regular control checks, e.g. stocktaking, cash counts. Often computers are used to cover up non-computer frauds. All frauds have a weak point in having to remove what has been taken (cash or other assets).

▪ Be aware that fraud might be occurring.
▪ Look out for signs that there may be problems: late payments, work backlogs, incomplete audit trails, people with an extravagant lifestyle, people who are 'experts', confused decision-making, multiple interlocking companies or deals, strange payments to countries with strict privacy laws, large transfers before public holidays.
▪ Don't look first for the complex: many frauds exploit simple missing elements of control.
▪ Look out for managers who say fraud can't happen in their department and say they have trustworthy staff.

Investigating fraud

The first step in investigating a fraud has to be to decide on the purpose of the investigation. There are several possibilities:

▪ gathering evidence for prosecution;
▪ confirming the extent of the fraud for audit purposes and/or for the purpose of gaining restitution;
▪ discovering how the fraud was committed and preventing its recurrence;
▪ attaching blame to those allowing the fraud to happen – possibly with a view to disciplinary action (or legal action if this is possible or advisable).

Which of these is most important will depend on the organisation and the situation. It is important to note that the standard of proof is normally higher for criminal actions (beyond reasonable doubt) than civil actions (the balance of probabilities). This means that if only restitution and/or dismissal is sought a lesser burden of proof is required than if the case needs to go to criminal court. You may be expected to discuss the relative importance of these elements for particular situations. Among the issues that might be important are:

▪ The size of the loss: a very large loss may significantly affect the operation of the company whereas a small loss may cost more to investigate than would be gained.
▪ The culture of the organisation and the country: it may be part of either culture that wrongdoing must always be prosecuted.
▪ The effect on the organisation's reputation: this might, for example, affect the confidence of customers or shareholders.
▪ Whether objectives conflict: it may be possible to get a conviction or recover money but not both.
▪ The effect of the investigation on the staff within the organisation.
▪ How far the fraud has injured parties other than the organisation: the Maxwell case, for example, had far-reaching implications for pensioners.

Just who should investigate fraud also needs to be discussed. Possible agencies are internal auditors, external auditors, the police, private investigators, etc. Just which will be involved will depend on the overall objectives decided. The audit committee (if one exists) should make the basic decision as to who carries out the investigation: indeed, this is a prime purpose of this committee. It may be sensible to put in a joint team of any of the agencies.

Any investigation is likely to have more than one of the objectives outlined above. Whichever objectives are set, it will be necessary to collect evidence by interviewing witnesses, interviewing suspects, analysing and acquiring documents and computer printouts, observation and other techniques. The investigation will have to cover all circumstances of the fraud and needs not just to seek out what happened but to try to establish why – both in terms of failure of internal control and in terms of motivation of the perpetrators.

The main problems for fraud investigation involve either evidence or people. Fraudsters often try hard to remove or destroy evidence, especially with computer fraud. The people problems relate to the motivation of witnesses and others. Some may wish to minimise their responsibility and distance themselves from the problem, others with something else to hide may also be unco-operative and yet others, in an effort to be 'helpful', may introduce false leads.

Few accountants encounter fraud themselves, though they may have heard about it from acquaintances. A good source of material is Michael J Comer's book on corporate fraud.

However, fraud is fairly frequent in industries where sales revenue is in cash and there are often a large number of small branch establishments.

4.9 Some methods used in quality assurance

This section explains and discusses some of the more important methods used in quality assurance and internal audit work.

Recording of information – flow charts

One of the important methods of working for internal auditors is to record the operation of various systems and subsystems within the organisation. In order to do this the internal auditor must make use of the very best tools for recording these systems. Though it is possible to record the systems using verbal descriptions an internal auditor must be able to use and create appropriate flow charts as required. There is inadequate space here to describe in detail the wide variety of flowchart techniques that are available.

A flow chart is a diagrammatic representation of the flow of something (information, data, document, activity, function) and the sequence of operations in a system or process. All flow charts have several purposes:

- analysis/description of existing system;
- criticism of system (especially in internal control);
- organising the design of a new system.

Examples of flow charts

- Data flow diagram: Documents *logical* flow of data through a system (compared with other flows).
- Procedure flow chart: Main purpose is to show *procedures* carried out and by *whom*.
- Program flow chart: (Used mainly in computer science/ programming). Portrays sequential and logical operations performed by a computer program.
- Document flow chart: To illustrate the control and flow of *documents* (and sometimes physical resources) between areas of responsibility in an organisation or system.
- Structure chart/ HIPO chart (Hierarchy plus Input, Process, Output). Diagram of functions performed by system: blueprint for computer code.
- System flow chart: A high-level description of major elements of a system, computerised or manual.
- Audit system flow chart: Similar to system flow charts, though symbols differ.

Each has:

- a specific (restricted) purpose;
- its own set of symbols (though there are some elements in common);
- its own style of presentation.

Flow charts have some distinct advantages over alternative methods of recording. These include the following:

- They are a formal model. This forces precise description of the system under scrutiny more perhaps than a descriptive approach.
- As a result they are rigorous and this rigour identifies inconsistencies and problems.
- They provide a permanent record of the system.
- They are visual, a factor which means they are often easier to understand and criticise than the written word.
- They are easy to update.

Flow charts are, like many other areas of internal auditing, much easier to prepare with the advent of computer technology. Flowcharting packages are readily available and make a more professional-looking chart very quickly. Among the major advantages of these over manual charts is their ease of amendment and automated linkage features. Some programming packages allow the use of a flowchart approach to writing computer programs.

Flowcharting, the precise description and analysis of systems, is the basis of most internal audit work. It is not sensible to comment on systems without being very clear about their nature and workings.

This has become easier in that virtually all systems in large organisations are computer systems and will have been flowcharted as part of the basic system design.

Problems tend not to arise with the standard processing of standard transactions. It would be alarming if the basic routine for the majority of transactions was unsound.

Problems normally arise in:

- attempts to process non-standard transactions in standard ways;
- new forms of transactions for which the system is insufficiently adapted;
- handling of exceptional items.

Sampling in internal audit

One of the problems of auditing (or internal auditing) any organisation, other than the very small, is that of dealing with many transactions. As most internal audit functions are limited by resource constraints, it is almost inevitable that some form of selection or sampling of items for study must be done. It is therefore crucial that internal auditors understand what is involved in sample selection and that statistical techniques are correctly applied. Besides this basic function of making internal audit manageable within resource constraints, sampling has a number of distinct advantages for the internal auditor. These include the following:

- Sampling can provide a very rapid view of the overall position, especially where there are large numbers of similar transactions.
- In many areas of auditing there is no need for a 100 per cent exact check, merely an overview of whether or not a procedure is working correctly. Checking of a statistically representative sample of a population can give a very quick and accurate view of the overall population characteristics.
- If early sampling begins to produce unacceptable errors, then more detailed checking can take place.
- Because sampling provides a quick method of arriving at conclusions, a wider range of tests can be undertaken and thus improve the quality of the work done.

There are, of course, disadvantages to sampling:

- Any form of sampling introduces the possibility of error. Though this may be measurable statistically, it is still present.
- As with any mathematical method, sampling must be used carefully within its limitations. If it is not then the method may be unreliable.

Sampling ideas

When only a small proportion of population (of transactions or accounts or balances) is taken the sampler must be interested in a number of key areas:

- The sample should contain the necessary phenomenon that is being investigated. In broad terms this means that the sample must be taken from the population and be representative of that population.
- Samples should be large enough to enable the phenomenon to be studied. A sample that is too small may simply miss the very phenomenon that is being

studied.

- As far as possible, the sample should be cost-beneficial, bearing in mind the aims of the investigation.
- Sampling should give an indication of the level of confidence that we have in any particular observation. The level of confidence that we can have from sampling can never be 100 per cent but we must be able to give some indication of how confident we are, based on the sample used.

In the rest of this section two distinct aspects of sampling are discussed. In the first section we explain the purpose and approach of sampling methods. The second section discusses the method of choosing a sample.

Methods of sampling

Figure 4.4 indicates the relationships between sampling methods.

Figure 4.4: Sampling methods

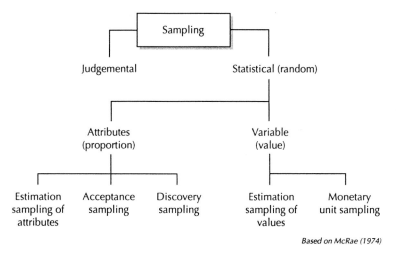

Based on McRae (1974)

The major distinction in sampling is between judgemental sampling and statistical sampling. *Judgemental* sampling is *not* statistical or random sampling and simply involves the auditor taking a view of which items should be included in the sample. Although this method is widely used, it is probably unacceptable for many purposes as it is not possible to draw any statistical inferences from the results. There are some circumstances where judgemental sampling may be adequate – for example, where a significantly large percentage of the population, in value terms, is examined in detail and judgemental sampling is used simply to give an indication of a minor part of the work. Judgement sampling is an effective form of discovery sampling – if errors/problems are quickly found. Experienced auditors can often do this by looking at transactions which represent potential errors – returns, disputes with customers. But if they fail to find anything there is no basis of a statistically valid sample to enable the auditor to say that there is a low probability of an error.

While statistical sampling should be used wherever possible, it should be recognised that in practice some non-statistical sampling is done, and can be justified where the cost and inconvenience of setting up proper sampling is excessive. An example of this is where there is a large quantity of unnumbered source documents. However, the internal auditor is not then entitled to draw quantitative conclusions from the sample, but can draw qualitative conclusions. The percentage of errors would not be validly estimated, but the causes of errors could be investigated to understand possible system defects.

Statistical sampling involves the use of statistical methods to decide how samples should be chosen and how results should be interpreted. Statistical sampling in auditing is broadly split into *attribute* sampling and *variable* sampling. Attribute sampling is used to estimate the proportion of items in a population which have a particular attribute of interest. Normally this attribute is an error or error condition. Attribute sampling effectively divides the population into two: those having the characteristic and those not having it. It is for this reason that the binomial distribution is used in this area.

Attribute sampling can be used in several different circumstances and three are shown in Figure 4.4. Each of these three is aimed at finding out about errors within the population but for three different purposes. *Estimation* sampling of attributes attempts to determine the percentage of items within the sample which are in error. This method can therefore be used to produce an observation such as *'based on sampling, we are 95 per cent certain that no more than 5 per cent of all sales invoices passed in a single month have errors'*. This particular method of sampling needs a fairly large sample size. *Acceptance* sampling would be used to estimate whether or not the level of errors in the population exceeded a given percentage (while not rejecting too many acceptable units). This method tries to estimate the chance that the error is greater than that set. Finally, *discovery* sampling is similar to acceptance sampling except that in this case *only if no errors are found* will the auditor accept the population error rate as being the accepted rate. These last two methods both need smaller sample sizes than estimation sampling, for comparable error percentages.

These are the main sampling approaches used in internal audit. Discovery sampling is used to demonstrate the possibility of system error; one error in a critical system can be enough to force revision. Estimation sampling of attributes is the main surveying method.

The population size is only one of a number of factors that affect the sample size that needs to be taken. Four factors affect the size of attribute samples:

- Population size: this is not a very important factor because, once a random sample has been chosen and representativeness obtained of a good cross-section, few additional items are needed, regardless of population size.
- The desired upper precision limit: this is the precision required by the auditor and will depend on the limit that the auditor was prepared to accept.
- The desired confidence level: this would normally be set at some fairly high level such as 90 or 95 per cent. The level will depend on the auditor's assessment of the risk of missing something. The overall audit risk can be broken down as follows:

Audit risk = Control risk × Inherent risk × Detection (sampling) risk

The exact confidence level will depend on the prior expectations of the auditor. These may be influenced by previous work done by the auditor, e.g. previous audits or checks on the internal control system.

- An advanced estimate of the population error rate: this may be gained by making a small preliminary survey or taking previous estimate from this population.

These factors can be combined with tables to identify the relevant sample size necessary for a particular assurance rate. The sample size would increase if either:

- the desired confidence level increased;
- the upper precision limit decreased;
- the population error rate increased;
- the population size increased.

Most texts provide a range of tables, which can be inspected to observe the range of variation. Best practice now is to use the formulae on which the tables are based in special audit software with a laptop PC.

The second major type of statistical test is *variable* sampling. For auditing purposes the main objective of this method is to estimate the true value of an account balance or similar total. This is the approach used by external auditors to support the balance sheet audit. It is not as appropriate as the estimation sampling of attributes to support the systems audit that is the main part of internal audit work, but it is important to understand the system to understand the basis of external audit work and because it can be useful in special investigations and in the review of new projects and acquisitions. There are two distinct sorts of variable sampling: *estimation* sampling and *monetary unit* sampling. Estimation sampling of variables is similar to attribute sampling except that the estimate produced is one of value rather than error rate. Using this method it is possible, for example, to estimate the total value of inventory based on the sample and compare this with the total inventory shown in the accounts. The mechanism of estimation sampling relies on the use of the relationship between the sample standard deviation and the population standard deviation. A major complicating factor with variable sampling is that it is unclear what the population distribution will be like. Examples of population distributions which may be found are shown in Figure 4.5. Many distributions are skewed, such as that found at D (or more rarely E).

As an example, sales invoices may start out as distribution A – errors in original pricing, extensions, etc. When reviewed some months later customers will have found and complained about errors where they lose and a few customers will have advised errors where they would have gained. The residual errors are losses to the organisation and may take on a skewed form as D or E.

There are various techniques available to enable the auditor to make estimates of the population. These include using stratified sampling where the effect of skewness is reduced. In addition, statistical inference allows us to make predictions about the population such as the mean and standard deviation in certain confidence limits.

Figure 4.5: Population distributions

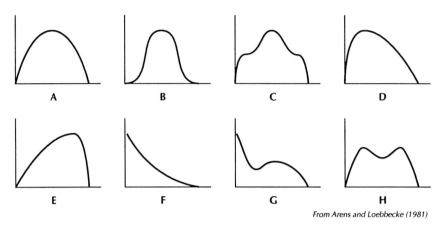

From Arens and Loebbecke (1981)

Monetary unit sampling (MUS) was initially developed by Haskins and Sells in 1961 and there are several variations of the original scheme in existence. The system attempts to measure error *value* and this is a value (compared with an attribute) sampling method. The required data for a MUS system is:

Total value of the population (e.g. of debtors)	V	(e.g. £100,000)
A reliability factor (based on a level of confidence)	R	(e.g. 2)
Monetary precision	P	(e.g. £500)

Sample size would then be calculated by taking $V \div (P \div R)$

The reliability factor is a translation, based on the value of λ in the cumulative Poisson distribution where $(x = 1)$. (λ is the average number of times a characteristic occurs, x is the number of occurrences.)

Thus:

Prior belief (e.g. in value of internal control system)	Confidence level required	Reliability factor (R)
Very good system	63%	1
Average system	86%	2
Poor system	95%	3

Intermediate levels of R can be calculated at intermediate points on the Poisson distribution.

Monetary precision is the specific value of the maximum acceptable error value. If an error exceeds this then it is regarded as significant for the investigation in hand. Some treatments of MUS link monetary precision with upper error limits and most likely error:

Monetary precision = Upper error limit – Most likely error

These figures are arrived at on the basis of judgement: there is no simple formula to assist. The key matter of concern here is materiality.

Therefore if the population value is £100,000, the reliability factor 2 and the minimum acceptable error is £500, then the sample interval is £500 ÷ 2 = £250 and the sample size is £100,000 ÷ £250 = 400. The novelty of MUS is to describe the sample in monetary units – £ or $ – and to use the sample size as a *sampling interval*. The population is listed to produce a cumulative currency value. A random starting point is chosen within the interval size (e.g. £239) and used as a starting-point. Then every 250th £ of the sample is noted and the observed unit in which it falls is selected for testing.

There are several important comments to be made about MUS.

- Any item with a value over the size of the sample interval is selected.
- Any item more than the value of the sample interval is selected more than once but will be audited only once.
- It assumes that the maximum amount by which an item may be in error will be the amount of the item: this is true for overstatement but not for understatement.
- The probability that an item will be selected is approximately equal to its value.
- A nil balance will never be selected for investigation.

Choosing samples

Whatever statistical sampling method is chosen the general idea is to obtain a representative sample and it is essential that such sampling is random. For random sampling to take place several conditions must hold:

- the population must be defined;
- the sampling unit must be defined;
- each possible sampling unit must have an equal chance of being selected;
- once an item is selected it must be treated as any other selected item and not later abandoned for inconvenience or some other factor;
- random sampling normally makes use of random number tables, though pseudo-random numbers created by computers may be equally acceptable.

Sometimes other selection methods are either more suitable or cheaper for a particular sample method. *Systematic selection* involves randomly establishing a starting-point and then selecting every *n*th record from the population up to the sample size. The major drawback of systematic selection is that it may not pick up systematic errors within the population. The major advantage of this method is its simplicity, particularly where computer audit tools are not being used.

Stratified selection may be used in situations where the population is known to be skewed. In this case the sampling of very large numbers of small items may produce little of material significance for the auditor and therefore not be worthwhile, whereas sampling of the larger items may be of more value.

Cluster sampling is where groups of units are selected where each cluster is randomly selected.

The main practical problems relate to defining the relevant population to ensure that it is a homogeneous population, and not two distinct populations. If wishing to test credit control systems, it is necessary to test customers and invoices where credit is sought. Customers who pay cash are irrelevant. The normal error is to assume that all of a population are similar, when there are quite distinct subgroups – but this becomes apparent from any significant preliminary work.

Working papers

Audit working papers need to be prepared by internal audit departments in the course of their work for three reasons:

- To provide a record of the work that has been done on any particular investigation as evidence for the conclusion to be reached.
- To provide a future reference when evidence is required of previous work done on the audit.
- To enable the work done by internal audit to be assessed.

Although working papers are required for many accounting functions, their evidential role in auditing generally has meant that many aspects of audit working papers have become quite formalised. This formalisation has led to the development of a number of standard formats of working papers, for example internal control questionnaires. Standard pro-formas can be useful: they reduce work load in preparation and are readily available. However, they have the disadvantage that the mere use of standard working papers may be insufficient for an adequate audit opinion. Standard working papers need to be adapted to suit the investigation being undertaken. There is a variety of listings of possible audit working papers, and that given in Figure 4.6 is typical. Working papers set out in this format will mirror the form of the report prepared and make for easy referencing should further information be required.

Figure 4.6: Working papers – possible contents

- The objectives of the particular investigation
- Details of past work in this area completed and outstanding and review of previous work
- The methods by which that investigation is being undertaken with possibly a timetable and details of the actions to be taken
- Details of the investigators involved with the particular problem
- Evidence collected, this being split as necessary into the various types of evidence including such matters as:
  (a) Copies of relevant management statements and memoranda
  (b) Details of statistical data and accounts
  (c) Internal control information, possibly including an internal control questionnaire
  (d) Copies of relevant correspondence
- A summary of significant matters reported and submissions made
- General conclusions and, if necessary, interpretations of the evidence collected
- Action proposed with reasons
- Conclusions and final report

(Source: Venables and Impey, 1991)

The exact content of working papers will depend on the particular investigation being undertaken and on the particular internal auditor concerned. As internal audit often undertakes investigations on a one-off basis, working papers for these tasks are likely to be somewhat varied. It is suggested, however, that all such working papers need to be constructed so as to include relevant items based around those in the table.

Often audit working papers are split into two separate files, the permanent file and the current file. The permanent file is for the underlying permanent or slowly changing details from the audit file and could contain details of rules and regulations of the organisation, extracts from minutes of meetings, details of systems and organisation charts, relevant legislation, and names and job descriptions of people involved in the particular investigation. The current file would contain details of specific investigations done at this audit, the results and any reports provided. For one-off investigations there may only be one file that contains both permanent and current data.

Working papers generally may contain the results of the use of tools and techniques which are mentioned below. Techniques which are of particular importance to internal audit are:

- analytical review;
- internal control questionnaires;
- testing;
- flow charts of all sorts: program, data, system, etc.;
- sundry system and decision description tools such as decision tables, Gantt charts and input–output tables.

In the changing environment with a greater demand for reassurance regarding internal control, there are increasing requirements for the review of internal audit. The working papers are the evidence of the work done and its quality, and should show:

- adherence to the audit philosophy and programme – adherence to internal audit policies and procedures, and any internal audit manual;
- any review should provide evidence of standardised working practices:
  - □ standard audit file layout
  - □ standardised techniques for flowcharting
  - □ standardised techniques for statistical sampling
  - □ standard working paper forms
  - □ adequate use of PCs, standard forms on disc, standard report layout, risk analysis from internal control evaluation questionnaires;
- evidence of the effects of reporting, management action and follow-up;
- evidence of the internal audit department's own procedures for supervising and monitoring the quality of work done.

Working papers are normally formalised, standardised, and prepared on laptop PCs. The basic working pattern now is that the internal auditor, working on an audit in any particular department, works, using standard tools and standard layouts, on his laptop PC, and at the end of the audit prints out reports in standard form and provides the internal audit department with all the working papers on disk. External audit work is largely done the same way.

Internal control questionnaires (ICQs)

ICQs are best thought of as detailed checklists of specific internal control techniques that should be present in a system for good internal control. ICQs can be developed in two ways: through adapting a generally available model ICQ or by developing one using an internal control evaluation questionnaire (ICEQ).

If a model ICQ is used, auditors need to take great care to adapt this to fit the particular circumstances of an organisation. This may mean merely omitting irrelevant sections but it may also mean adding sections for particular problems not envisaged in the general model.

Questions in an ICEQ are more general questions about control issues and are unlikely to have the yes/no answers typical of an ICQ. An ICEQ asks major questions (e.g. does the computer system management ensure that fraud cannot occur?) and an internal control questionnaire may then be developed from it to ask detailed questions, each of which can be given a yes/no answer within the general subject area of the ICEQ. The ICEQ can therefore be the development stage for the ICQ. There may be circumstances where the auditor is satisfied to use just the ICEQ, perhaps for a small business. The detailed ICQ is, however, probably a better tool on which to base an opinion.

ICQ advantages and disadvantages

Advantages	Disadvantages
Can cover most typical weaknesses in control	Questions don't differentiate between major and minor weaknesses
Provides a checklist for the auditor	Doesn't remove need for auditor judgement
Can be used in conjunction with flow-charting	ICQs may not suit the organisation and other tests exactly
Standard format helps with review	ICQs encourage mechanical replies
Quality control facilitated	
Provides objective data, provided questions are well thought out.	

With ICQs almost inevitably any responses that suggest lack of adequate control will lead to recommendations by the auditor for improvements. The lack of adequate control may also give rise to further actions such as:

- a decision that particular balances or accounts need further investigation to discover their validity (substantive tests); and/or
- a change in the accounts or provisions to reflect the problems uncovered.

This latter action is more likely to be related to external audit than internal audit.

ICQs are not without their critics. A summary of some of the advantages and disadvantages of ICQs is given in the table above (based on Venables and Impey, 1991).

One of the problems of reviewing and understanding internal audit is the apparent dependence in many areas, such as this, on checklists. This was originally a matter of enabling the use under supervision of junior staff, or staff who would spend only a limited time in internal audit (e.g. newly qualified accountants joining the organisation), and has become in the changing environment where internal audit itself has to be assessed (and audited) a way of proving that nothing material has been omitted from the work programme. It is easy to underestimate the judgement required in ensuring that the questions asked are the critical questions for the particular organisation, and in assessing the answers.

Risk analysis, discussed in the next section, based on ICQs and ICEQs has become a matter of formalising consistent judgement across all aspects of an organisation to ensure that the audit programme reflects and balances the relevant risks. Increasingly this is a matter of combining standard weightings for the various factors to achieve scores using special software to evaluate audit risk and control matrices. These approaches are described in Chambers (1992) and Chambers and Rand (1994).

Testing

Testing is probably the central process of most external and internal audit. The main purpose of any test is comparison between two items. Tests may be the comparison of, for example:

- the way an action is carried out with the way the action should have been carried out;
- an actual quantity with its actual recorded value;
- a conclusion compared with conclusions arrived at by other people.

There are two problems with testing in the internal audit field. One is measurement, especially where subjective measures are needed, e.g. where an opinion needs to be expressed.

The second area of problems relates to the cost-benefit of testing. Undoubtedly everything that needs to be tested could be tested, but there may be a point beyond which the cost of testing outweighs the benefit of testing. The discussion of this second problem leads us into sampling and materiality that are discussed in separate sections.

Several terms are used in audit in relation to audit tests. Two of the most common are *compliance* tests and *substantive* tests. Compliance tests mainly involve checking that a system's operation complies with a requirement or specification. Substantive tests seek to establish the validity of (or substantiate) certain items in the accounts.

In order to do a compliance test, the auditor must have a clear idea of what should happen and for this reason needs to have extensive knowledge of the required system. Testing can be undertaken in two specific ways:

- By ensuring that the system has operated correctly in relation to particular controls. It may thus be possible to check that payments have been authorised and cheques have been issued for the correct amount.
- By attempting to defeat the system. Such a test of the system may be undertaken using test transactions to identify the limits which the system will tolerate before identifying out of control situations.

Substantive tests are particularly done in relation to assets in the balance sheet but may also be done for items in the profit and loss account such as sales, sales returns and directors' emoluments. Substantive tests may also be undertaken in relation to other investigations such as fraud and value for money.

There is an obvious relationship between substantive and compliance testing. If compliance testing reveals the system works well, it is likely that the *outputs* of the system, e.g. the accounting statements, are accurate. This of course assumes that the system by which compliance tests have been done is itself capable of producing the required *outcomes*. Testing this involves investigating whether or not the system operates effectively: a value-for-money audit.

It should be remembered that the main business of internal audit is the review of the systems and their functioning. This work should in the main be compliance testing. In public-sector auditing the work of internal auditors is defined as compliance testing, not substantive testing, which is left to external audit.

Testing itself may be done using a number of different methods and these need to be selected according to the particular investigation and the company concerned. Among the methods that may find use are the following:

- questionnaires, for example internal control questionnaires;
- observation, especially where control produces no written records;
- checking of written documents (including computer files);
- physical measurement, especially in the case of inventory, physical quantities;
- test data sets, especially in computer environments;
- walk-through tests, especially where controls involve physical barriers and document scrutiny;
- interviews.

Whichever methods are used they should be used correctly, consistently and methodically with results (positive or negative) clearly recorded in working papers. Tests provide evidence for opinions in reports and their conclusions must be justifiable.

4.10   Planning and control of quality assurance

The work of the internal audit department needs to be planned in order to be efficient and cost-effective, and earlier sections have indicated the planning steps necessary in general. There are increasing pressures for improved planning of audits due to a variety of factors:

- Increased size of firms: this is producing more complex operations, often multinational. Internal audit may no longer be able to run from a single office or department, so co-ordination and planning become essential.
- Resources, particularly labour, are expensive. The increasing professionalism of internal audit means that salaries generally are growing. Thus efficiency demands that labour costs are minimised and labour use maximised.
- Competitive pressures mean that internal auditing must be shown to be cost-beneficial. This must be checked at the planning stage as far as possible. Many investigations intend to look into cost-benefit issues and they must themselves be cost-beneficial.
- Changing standards. Although accounting standards are a key area of internal audit concern, they are not the only ones: computer standards, health and safety at work, etc. are all possible concerns of the internal audit department in their various roles. As the standards change, the internal auditor must look at how previous work patterns are likely to change and must plan for these new patterns.
- Increased pressure for quality means that mistakes are likely to prove embarrassing and costly.

Planning in internal audit follows much the same pattern as planning generally: set objectives, decide how to pursue those objectives, select and allocate resources, prepare a detailed operating schedule, implement, report and review. The area of setting objectives is of special interest as it includes a discussion of risk assessment.

Objectives for some investigations may be set outside the internal audit department, especially for one-off investigations requested by the board or audit committee. The involvement of these in approving the overall programme for internal audit and one-off investigations should not be regarded as a formal matter of showing their concern for good governance; non-executive directors should be able to contribute a wider view of external change and how it may affect the operations of the organisation. Indications of possible objectives have already been given. There are situations where the internal audit department has a duty to undertake regular investigations into general control areas. For these it is essential that the planning process is informed by an analysis of where the most likely problems are and thus where the resources of the department would be best directed. In this situation assessment of materiality and risk are essential tools.

Materiality

The materiality concept is defined in the CIMA *Official Terminology* as:

> *Information is material if its omission or misstatement could influence the economic decisions of users taken on the basis of the financial statements. Materiality depends on the size of the item or error judged in the particular circumstances of its omission or misstatement. Thus materiality provides a cut-off point rather than being a primary qualitative characteristic that*

information must have if it is to be useful.

The Auditing Practices Board definition of materiality is:

In an accounting sense a matter is material if its non-disclosure, misstatement or omission would make possible a distortion of the view given by the accounts or other financial information.

The former definition is related especially to management accounting, the latter to external financial reporting. Both in essence indicate that materiality is about deciding what is significant, in terms of value, for an investigation or report. There may be different levels of materiality for different tasks.

Deciding on the appropriate level of materiality is important in the planning of an audit (as materiality directly affects the amount of work needing to be done), in audit testing (see, for example, the discussion on sampling above) and in reporting results: too low a level will cost a lot in time, possibly for little benefit, and too high a level may miss items of significance. Often materiality is expressed in relation to the total task being undertaken, e.g. 1 per cent of turnover or 0.5 per cent of the total asset value. The level of materiality is related to risk and different risks have given rise to different *forms of materiality*:

- Materiality by value: an expensive asset is more material than a low-value one.
- Materiality by nature of the risk involved: some transactions are more significant than others, e.g. items requiring mandatory disclosure may be very significant as may easily disposable assets and inventory (e.g. cash and diamonds).
- Materiality in reporting: in a report to the local manager smaller items will be significant whereas they will not be in reports to head office management.

The concept of materiality is relatively easy to explain. Its application is more difficult as it depends on judgement in a particular situation. A general rule is that if investigating, testing or reporting is likely to be differently viewed depending on the state of a particular item then that item is material.

The assessment and management of audit risk

Internal auditors must understand the concept of risk and how risk may be assessed in the planning of controls and audits within an organisation. Risk can be defined as *the chance of bad consequences or loss*. It is important primarily to understand what this means in relation to an organisation.

Generally the term risk would mean anything which is likely to cause the organisation to make a financial loss. This could include poor trading, market conditions, disasters, theft and mismanagement. This particular section discusses quality control of information systems and so the concept of risk in this context must be limited to loss by non-quality control.

Though there are many specific sorts of risk, these can probably be summarised in four main areas:

- disasters, outside the control of the organisation;
- errors, as a result of human or machine problems;
- mismanagement;
- misappropriation of resources, physical assets or tangible assets.

It must be one of the key roles of management generally to identify the risks faced by a particular business. The internal auditor, must also be able to identify the risks that are likely to be faced in the situation in which he/she is working.

The response to risk

Beaumont and Sutherland (1992) suggest that there are five important countermeasures against risk. These are:

- Transfer the risk: in particular, this means to undertake insurance which spreads the risk between different participants. Limited liability is another way of transferring risk.
- Reduce the probability of risk (chance that problems will occur): this can be undertaken by the introduction of controls such as having two signatures and/or a maximum level on payments.
- Reduce the vulnerability (or exposure) to risk: in a trading situation this can be done by removing the company from risky situations (e.g. don't make any local payments at branches).
- Detect the occurrence: this is achieved by the implementation of protection controls that are listed elsewhere under the general control framework.
- Enable recovery: this must be accomplished by the implementation of recovery procedures appropriate to the situation. These could include computer disaster recovery plans, relocation plans, etc.

The internal auditor, as part of the internal control system, is involved in ensuring that these controls and other countermeasures against risk are operating correctly. However, the internal auditor is only too well aware that there is a further secondary risk that the countermeasures themselves will not be operative. It is at this second level that most audit textbooks take up the risk analysis scenario.

The assessment of risk

The auditor usually classifies the risks we have discussed up to this point (that are controlled by the countermeasures against those risks) as *inherent* risks. There is a second set of risks: that the controls are not working. These risks are called *control* risks. The auditor is also concerned with *detection* risk, which is the chance that the auditor does not detect risks through substantive tests. Both control and detection risks may involve:

- *sampling* risk that results from testing one sample rather than another; and
- *non-sampling* risk that relates to all risks in audit testing not specifically related to sampling.

Overall audit risk facing the auditor comprises inherent risk, control risk and detection risk. These are normally described using a formula intended to derive overall risk thus:

Audit risk = Inherent risk × Control risk × Detection risk

This formula may be used to discover overall audit risk by estimating risk of each element. Thus, if inherent risk is 50 per cent, control risk 25 per cent and detection risk 30 per cent, then the overall risk is 3.75 per cent (0.5 × 0.25 × 0.3). This is a useful idea, though it may be dangerous to use subjective probabilities in this purely mechanical way.

Venables and Impey (p.134) describe audit risk as the risk 'accepted by an auditor that an invalid conclusion will be drawn *after* completion of all audit procedures' (emphasis added). This seems to imply that it is the *residual* risk after testing, not the overall risk. This overall pattern of risk, control and the internal auditor is expressed graphically in Figure 4.7.

Figure 4.7: Risk, control and the internal auditor

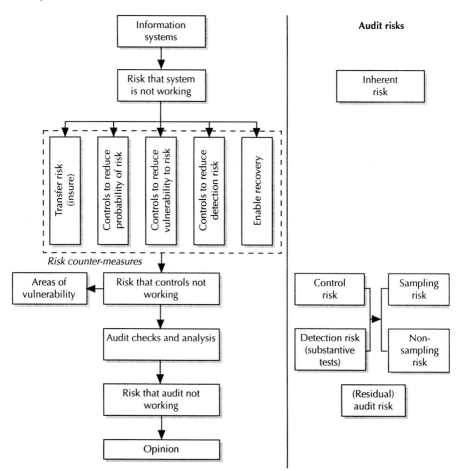

It is important for auditors to understand what risk is involved at each stage of an investigation and to give some indication of the size and probability of that risk. Inevitably this information will be subjective. Both risk and probability are extremely difficult to identify and measure and auditors are well aware of this. However, some assessment of risk is needed for several reasons:

▪ to see whether risk is sufficiently high to warrant investigation of a particular area;
▪ to decide among priorities for internal audit work in relation to the risk which is faced by different areas;
▪ to estimate the level of resources that it is worth putting into a particular audit situation.

The main approach to risk analysis for auditors is the use of *risk indexing*. This is an approach that attempts to:

▪ assess the various factors involved in risk;
▪ attach numeric weights to these factors that indicate the extent to which one risk is higher or lower than another;
▪ to sum these to give an overall assessment of risk.

The resulting index numbers are only subjective (scalar) assessments and should be interpreted with care. However, the technique does provide useful information in allowing comparison of different audit risks.

One method is to create a list of concern items, each of which represents particular areas vulnerable to risk (see Figure 4.8). For each item, an indication is provided of exposure (monetary value), vulnerability (likelihood of loss) and internal control effectiveness (control assessment). Each of these three indicators may be given a very simple index value, say one to three (or one to five), depending on the auditor's judgement of that area. A risk analysis index can then be either the sum or the product of these three numbers (the example below shows the product) to indicate which areas would be the most worthwhile pursuing.

Figure 4.8: Example list

Item of concern	Value £000	Exposure (3, 2, or 1) (value-based)	Vulnerability (3, 2 or 1)	Internal control effectiveness (1–5)	Product
		(a)	(b)	(c)	(a × b × c)
1 Fixed assets	2,000	2	2	2	8
2 Creditors	5,000	3	1	4	12
3 Factory WIP	2,000	2	2	3	12
4 Cash	500	1	3	1	3
5 Investments	5,000	3	2	1	6
Overall total					41

If this analysis is repeated for three or four areas the overall index for each area can give a relative view of risk in order to compare the situations. The areas with the highest overall totals will become the priority in that audit, and similarly the items within each area with the highest index will become priorities in that area.

Among factors which are included in a risk assessment might be:

- Financial indicators. These will be particularly used to indicate the size of the potential risk. Monetary values themselves might not be used in the index calculation, but rather an index of relative value in relation to the total audit problem.
- The nature and style of management. What is of concern here is the ability of management to manage, and thus a scalar approach is all that is possible. Measurement of this is extremely difficult, and might involve looking at a number of different indicators such as staff turnover, staff development, innovation, control, quality of internal controls and so on.
- The nature of the operation. Of importance here might be the complexity of the operation, its position within the overall management of the organisation, and its strategic importance to the firm.
- The operation of internal controls. As the internal auditor is looking at the potential failure of internal controls, the ability of the controls to operate is crucially important in the assessment of risk.

The information needed for risk assessments may be gleaned from a variety of sources. These would include past internal audits, initial and existing contact with the part of the organisation concerned, past history including the reason for this particular audit being requested, exploratory audits and information gleaned from the informal information system within the organisation.

The way this information is incorporated into an overall judgement will depend on the past experience of the auditor. This experience will provide the basis of what is known to give a sound judgement. Different companies use different methods to greater or lesser effect. The main point of risk analysis is to obtain consistency of judgement across different situations and time periods.

Though these risk analysis methods are intended to help with the allocation of resources, they do not themselves include an indicator of resource requirement for each area. It is, however, important that when risk analysis is used potential costs as well as the potential benefit in reducing risk are identified.

Chambers explains how the process of risk assessment for audit planning is becoming a matter of appropriate computer models and matrices to ensure systematic evaluation and aid consistent judgement.

The Chambers approach is valuable to enable relative risk to be assessed, comparing judgements and attempting to be consistent. It is hence very useful as a preliminary stage of planning internal audit and the distribution of finite resources in skilled staff over problem areas. It is also very useful in clarifying views on potential risk – the amount that could be at stake if there were major problems or system deficiencies.

But it does not remove the need for intelligent judgement of potential problems based on knowledge and experience. Auditors need to be able to review potential audit areas and identify key issues and make provisional assessments of risk to plan preliminary audits, using what is known of areas from previous work and what can be deduced from analytical review and risk exposure analysis.

Conclusion

This long section has explained the developing requirements for assurance concerning internal control. These have become considerably more complex in recent years with a wider range of interested parties, and far greater control risks with a rapidly changing environment, and new technology, financial systems and markets.

Management has always required assurance regarding the effectiveness of internal control, and this has been provided by internal audit, which has been the source of independent advice to management.

Internal audit developed, using similar techniques to external audit, but emphasising the systems audit. It has to change to recognise its new status as the source of the evidence of reasonable assurance that directors must provide to shareholders and other users of accounts regarding internal control.

It also has to change and possibly develop new techniques to provide appropriate assurance in a changing environment. An example of this could be the internal audit of the treasury function and the use of derivatives.

5 Comparative Governance Models

From Alex Dunlop, 'Corporate accountability: more form than substance?', in K Smith and P Johnson (eds), *Business Ethics and Business Behaviour*, International Thomson Business Press, 1996.

With the spread of British influence around the world in Victorian and Edwardian times, it was natural that British systems of corporate governance would follow. Consequently, they became the basis for company legislation in colonies such as India, Hong Kong, Singapore, South Africa, New Zealand, Australia and Canada. Although developments in the USA were not so directly influenced by British precedents, there were sufficient similarities in national approaches to the recognition of individual freedoms that the systems adopted contain a high degree of similarity. Individual states passed legislation during the nineteenth century to facilitate the incorporation of companies. Governance was again through the members' meeting, which had the power to nominate and elect the directors and to require regular accountability from them. Federal incorporation was not, and is still not, available.

Developments in continental Europe followed a different path, reflecting, again, the differing cultural norms. The regulation of corporate entities in Germany adopted a far more prescriptive and tightly controlled model, which lacked the flexibility of British common law. Shareholders' interests were represented and protected by a supervisory board, quite separate from the management of the company. The supervisory board annually examined and reported on the financial statements prepared by the management directors. Moreover, they could call meetings of the members and, if cause was shown, change the management. It could, therefore, be argued (Tricker, 1990) that top management in German companies is subject to greater independent scrutiny than their counterparts in this country – a criticism which would have been redressed if the European Community's Fifth Draft Company Law Directive had been adopted, as it originally called for the two-tier, supervisory form of governance, instead of the unitary board with executive and non-executive directors, for all public companies registered in the member states.

In France, the 1807 Napoleonic Code provided the basis for company law, which was consequently prescriptive, providing detailed rules for the conduct of corporate affairs. In 1863 the Société à Responsabilité Limitée was created for companies with capital up to 20 million francs, giving limited liability to both managing (who had previously been excluded) and outside shareholders. The size restriction was subsequently removed.

In Japan, according to Nobes and Parker (1991), the first commercial code was established in 1899, based on the prescriptive Franco-German model and oriented towards creditors and tax collection. Until at least the Second World War, the Japanese economy was dominated by a small number of Zaibatsu, industrial–political consortia, usually involving a bank and originally based on noble families. The importance of banks in the system and the existence of somewhat feudal aspects of business control still survive.

The most common form of business organisation in Japan is the Kabushiki Kaisha, which is similar in many respects to the public limited company in the UK. The liability of shareholders is limited to the amount of the subscribed nominal capital, a benefit which requires compliance with the requirements for publicly accessible financial reporting. In addition, the Ministry of Finance administers the Securities and Exchange Law, which applies only to those Kabushiki Kaisha whose shares are publicly traded.

The Securities and Exchange Law was enacted shortly after the Second World War, when General MacArthur was responsible for the Allied administration of Japan. The MacArthur regime naturally adopted the US system of corporate regulation as the model for the revised Japanese system. Consequently, the functions and powers of the Ministry of Finance in relation to financial reporting and corporate control are similar in many respects to those of the US Securities and Exchange Commission, although there is not a directly equivalent body in Japan.

5.1 The US perspective

Life in the New World, through the eyes of leaders, following the War of Independence, as described by Monks and Minow (1991), was based on a suspicion of power. This concern manifested itself in the development of an elaborate written constitution explicitly designed to balance different potential elements of power against each other.

The colonial-era citizens were, however, familiar with the concept of the corporation. Indeed, the early colonies began their existence in the form of joint stock companies. The earliest history of the Massachusetts Bay and Plymouth companies demonstrates the evolution of governmental powers from a commercial charter. Thus, corporations themselves were not suspect – what was essential was that the corporate form be available on a free and open basis.

The constitution, however, makes no mention of the word 'corporation' and it and its attendant Bill of Rights did not easily cater for the rights of these 'artificial citizens'. As recently as 1990, the Supreme Court was still trying to decide how the protections of the Bill apply to corporations. On the one hand, the American tradition of denying express power to government encouraged the belief that power granted to corporations would further the interests of the individual against the state. On the other, the same year that the USA declared its independence, Adam Smith was writing in the *Wealth of Nations* that directors of publicly held corporations could not be expected to watch the company

> with the same anxious vigilance with which the partners in a private copartnery frequently watch over their own.... Negligence and profusion,

therefore, must always prevail, more or less, in the management of such a company.

Louis Brandeis (1933) warned that it was a mistake to 'accept the evils attendant upon the free and unrestricted use of the corporate mechanism as if these evils were the unescapable price of civilised life'. He continued:

Incorporation for business was commonly denied long after it had been freely granted for religious, educational and charitable purposes. It was denied because of fear. Fear of encroachments upon the liberties and opportunities of the individual. Fear of the subjection of labour to capital. Fear of monopoly. Fear that the absorption of capital by corporations, and their perpetual life, might bring evils similar to those which attended mortmain. There was a sense of some insidious menace inherent in large aggregations of capital, particularly when held by corporations.

To resolve these concerns, an essential part of the system was a kind of corporate democracy, with each 'citizen' entitled to vote according to his investment. If government were permitted to exercise public power through the accountability imposed by the electoral system, it would be logical to permit corporations to exercise private power on the same basis.

It was this involvement of the shareholder/owner in the decision-making process which imbued the corporate system with its validity as being a reasonable representation of the public will. The famous statement of former General Motors president, Charlie Wilson, at his confirmation hearing for Secretary for Defence, was uttered with absolute conviction: 'For years I thought what was good for the country was good for General Motors, and vice versa.' The frequent potential conflicts of interest were becoming more and more apparent as big business grew bigger and began to take on a stance of its own. Commentators began to attribute the US's faltering international competitiveness to a dysfunction in the corporate system, a system which until then had served the country so well.

According to Monks and Minow (1991), the aspects of the system designed to help the corporation preserve itself have worked, but the aspects of the system designed to make sure that its self-preservation was consistent with the public interest have not. Government, boards of directors and even the market-place itself, have all been unable to keep the interests of the corporation aligned with those of the community, or, to put it another way, to keep it from making everyone else pay the costs of its profits.

This dysfunction was evidenced during the 1980s by the violence in the market for corporate control, with corporate raiders and leveraged buy-out (LBO) specialists adopting a cavalier approach to 'liberating' shareholder value, by buying out traditional shareholders and restructuring corporations.

5.2 Pressures on corporate accountability

It can be argued that the massive use of the corporate form in modern times must provide vindication for the robustness and flexibility of the system (Tricker, 1990) – this would be, however, to ignore the countless instances when the very system has proved to be less than satisfactory in the resolution of competing claims on corporate assets or within the corporate power base. The problems, it appears, become more difficult to manage the bigger the corporation becomes.

British Petroleum plc has in excess of 550,000 registered shareholders, many other public companies have more than 100,000 shareholders, and it would be difficult to find a member of the FT-SE 100 with less than 20,000. Control in the British company rests firmly with the shareholder – but how can 100,000 shareholders arrive at a reasoned, objective, collective decision? There is bound to be a widely differing level of knowledge and understanding of corporate and financial affairs, differing levels of interest in them, differing perspectives, from the potential short-term gain to longer-term investment security and annual income.

At this level, for the company just to be able to communicate effectively with its shareholders is an achievement in itself – for shareholders to communicate with each other in an effective manner is virtually impossible. Hence the development of widely known and understood corporate reporting codes and signals, such as earnings per share (EPS), price/ earnings ratios (P/E), return on capital employed (ROCE) and dividend yields: in other words, utilisation of a series of common denominators, on which are based major decisions about a corporation's future.

Should a shareholder wish to become more informed as to the status of a shareholding, it will involve reading and understanding complex reports containing large volumes of high-level financial information; either that or making use of professional analysts and commentators who, in general, may well have access to more relevant information, obtained from first-hand dealings with the company, and which could give some insight into the all-important dimension, usually omitted, relating to the company's future operating prospects.

These problems of communication and understanding do not, of course, exist at all levels of corporate activity. The vast majority of incorporated entities in this country (and the others which have adopted comparable systems) are smaller, privately owned companies, where the prime motivation for incorporation was to seek the protection of limited liability, rather than a means of accessing larger-scale capital markets. There are fewer problems of communication and understanding, growth is more likely to be financed from retained earnings, and the transfer of ownership on succession is facilitated.

It is, however, on the activities of the larger corporate entity that attention is most frequently focused. Apart from the already mentioned problems of communication and control, the prescribed legal structure can cause operational difficulties. All major enterprises now trade through a group of subsidiary and associated companies. In some cases these groups are relatively simple, with a small hierarchy of wholly-owned companies under a common parent company. In other cases, groups can be exceedingly complex, with many companies wholly or partly held at many levels in the network, with cross-holdings of shares between group companies, minority interests in such companies and with cross-directorships, intragroup transactions and other interdependencies.

It is common for group structures to be designed to facilitate management control, or for international tax planning purposes, to limit financial disclosure, to extend the limitation of liability, or for other regulatory reasons (Tricker, 1990): in such cases, management control structures can fit uneasily into legally prescribed formats, causing operating and control inefficiencies.

To a large extent, these aspects can be considered technicalities which can be managed by the use of appropriate devices – the main problem continues to lie elsewhere. According to Michael Jensen (1989) it is the continuing conflict of interest between boards of directors and shareholders which puts the very long-term future of the public corporation at risk.

Its genius is rooted in its capacity to spread financial risk over the diversified portfolios of thousands of individuals and institutions and to allow investors to customise risk to their own circumstances and predilections. By diversifying risks that would otherwise have been borne by owner-entrepreneurs and by facilitating the creation of a liquid market for exchanging risk, the public corporation has lowered the cost of capital.

This ability to quickly garner large amounts of investment capital and to spread the portfolio risk over large numbers is likely to continue to be useful, particularly in the cases of companies operating in growth industries, such as computers and electronics, biotechnology, pharmaceuticals and financial services. In these cases, companies are likely to be able to choose from among a surplus of potentially profitable projects and unlikely to systematically choose unprofitable ones.

The real problem for the public corporation to resolve is where it is operating in a mature industry, where long-term growth is likely to be low. In such cases, internally generated funds can easily outstrip the opportunities to invest them profitably, or where changes in technology or markets dictate a switching of resources to alternative products or projects.

Industries falling into this category might well include steel, chemicals, brewing, tobacco, wood and paper products. In these and other cash-rich, low-growth or declining sectors, there are often great, sometimes insidious, pressures on management to dissipate cash flow through investment in risky or unsound projects, or just through organisational inertia.

Managers have incentives to retain rather than distribute cash, partly because cash reserves increase their autonomy *vis-à-vis* the capital markets; this can sometimes serve a competitive purpose, but there is a tendency towards ineffective use and inertia. Cash distributions are also resisted for other less than accountable reasons – retaining cash increases the size of the company, a factor which appears to play an important part in the determination of executive remuneration (which in itself is a source of much shareholder unrest) and social prominence.

A radical approach is put forward by Jensen as a possible solution to this corporate malaise – the replacement of equity by debt (borrowings). Debt is said to be a powerful instrument for change and for instilling greater efficiency into corporations and for creating greater shareholder value. Borrowing commits managers to pay out future cash flows to the providers of capital and removes the element of discretion. To a large extent, what he is recommending is something of a validation of a process which had been having a major impact on corporate USA for a large part of the 1980s – the arrival of the LBO and the LBO association.

The intensive use of debt dramatically shrinks the amount of equity necessary within a company, and it is, therefore, possible to concentrate ownership holdings without the previously attendant requirement to commit large amounts of permanent equity capital. To a great extent, the necessity of the largest funding source taking the form of debt has the effect of transferring the risk diversification process to it, rather than leaving it with the equity.

Arranging these high-yielding (high-risk) securities became the province of a few well-known specialist firms, the best known of which was the now deceased Drexel Burnham Lambert which employed the most famous dealer, Michael Milken. The process of portfolio risk diversification, previously applied to equity investments, was supposed to apply in a similar manner to these new debt securities, particularly when the diversification process was considered at its secondary level in the holdings of the ultimate investors in the pension and mutual funds themselves.

Issue was taken with Jensen's contentions, most notably by Rappaport (1990), who emphasised the necessity for corporate entities to have long-term planning horizons in order to retain the confidence of customers, suppliers and employees.

He also recommended the adoption by companies of an institutionalised approach to shareholder value, which would result in at least similar performance improvements to those claimed of LBOs. In any event, these recent developments have had the effect of increasing institutional involvement in corporate affairs, and Jensen went so far as to draw comparisons between what was happening with LBO associations in the USA with the Japanese keiretsu business groupings.

5.3 The German and Japanese perspectives

The foregoing analogy was based on the similarities with the substantial bank holdings of debt and equity in large Japanese corporations, and the long-term involvement of the banks and designated executives in corporate strategies and problem-solving.

The Japanese Commercial Code requires a Kabushiki to have at least three directors (torishimariyaku), who are elected by the shareholder members. The board of the typical Kabushiki, however, is much larger, with 25–35 being quite normal, and 50 or more not unknown. The composition of a Japanese board is markedly different from a typical western one, in that it is made up almost entirely of inside, executive directors, with no involvement from independent, outside ones.

Moreover, its mode of operation is essentially hierarchical, unlike the US/UK model, which is based on equal responsibility. Indeed, the typical board represents the top three or four echelons of the corporate organisational pyramid.

The chairman is the most senior representative director and meets with his opposite numbers from other firms in the industry, and fosters relations with government through personal links with politicians. The president is the top operating officer in the corporation. Eventually he would expect to become chairman, a position with considerable honour. The representative directors are the most senior members of the board, which directs the activities of the company, supervising the performance of the managing directors, who might head up divisions, with the directors under them heading up subdivisions. Toyota, for example, has had five representative directors, ten managing directors and 33 directors.

With the corporation seen as a social unit and with a consensus approach to decision-making, there is no call for outside directors, who would not be part of the social network; nor would there be a place for them within the board's executive, and extremely competitive, hierarchy. The case for independent board membership to provide a system of checks and balances is less apparent given life-time employment and loyalty to the company evidenced by the humiliation of dismissal.

Due to the stability of bank and institutional shareholding and industrial cross-holdings, there has been little merger and acquisition activity, although this is now increasing. Consequently, directors have not had to be concerned about prospective predators, nor have boards been under pressure from outside interests seeking representation. Unlike the notion of shareholder democracy in the western model, with members voting for nominated directors, at the Japanese shareholders' meeting, approval for newly promoted directors is typically shown by a round of applause!

Ironically, however, this much lauded Japanese system, said to encourage stability and the long-term view, is undergoing dramatic change. Japanese corporations have been so commercially successful in their global product markets over the last two decades that they have generated substantial cash resources and have thus been able to reduce their dependence on their traditional sources of bank funding. Also, the emergence of sophisticated international funds markets, particularly the Eurobond, has enabled Japanese companies to even reduce dependence on their domestic market for funding.

In addition, in the last few years, the Japanese stock market has not been performing well, which has caused banks and insurance companies to offload poor-performing shares, due to concern about capital–adequacy ratios and returns for policyholders. This has, in turn, introduced a greater element of liquidity into the market for equities.

There is also evidence that the pace of product market-led change will have an impact on the structure of Japanese industry – the composition of the top 100 companies is changing quite substantially: in each of the last two decades, 20 firms were displaced and only one firm in three has remained even as long as 30 years. Many of the industries which currently have Japanese domination are maturing and Japanese corporations will be required to downsize, divest and restructure to remain competitive, again introducing substantial elements of change.

They would, thus, appear to be moving towards more of a US/UK approach to corporate funding, which, if these trends continue, will eventually lead to similar problems of investor accountability which currently beset the first two countries.

The German system for funding corporate enterprises has been described as heavily bank-based and has been endowed with similar beneficially stabilising, long-term attributes to the Japanese system: but do such circumstances actually exist, and, if so, are they also likely to come under major pressures which will cause change to take place? These were some of the questions investigated by Edwards and Fischer (1991) and in respect of which their findings were quite surprising.

Owing to the difficulties in obtaining directly comparable financial information in the UK, mainly because of the fact that in Germany all assets are required to be included in financial statements at historical cost, whereas in the UK it is relatively common for land and buildings to be revalued, usually resulting in a corresponding uplift to shareholders' capital, they used sources and uses of funds data for the period 1960–89 to carry out their evaluation.

They found that by far the largest source of corporate funding during the period was retained profits, with the 1980–9 period showing 85 per cent of the total deriving from this category and only 12.6 per cent being provided by long-term bank borrowings, a figure which is less than the UK level of around 20 per cent.

They then went on to look at the nature of bank lending in Germany, compared with the UK. A characteristic of the German system is claimed to be the existence of housebanks, whereby individual companies use one large bank which provides most of their financial requirements and acts as lead bank whenever syndicated credits and other facilities are required. Also the presence of representatives of these banks on supervisory boards is argued to reduce the extent of information asymmetry between borrowers and lenders, so that bank loans are available on more favourable terms than in the UK.

A further consequence of these relationships is said to be that the banks will be more supportive of companies in financial distress than would be the case in the UK, due to the fact that it would be possible to have this risk-taking compensated for in future and not eroded by competition from other banks. German banks are also seen to be better equipped to handle funding requirements, due to the existence of sizeable staffs of technical advisers, well versed in the assessment of industrial prospects and risks.

Almost all these preconceptions about German banking relationships were found to be misplaced. The banks do not, in fact, have specialist departments which have the technical expertise to assess whether particular projects for which finance is being sought are likely to be successful. Neither is bank representation on supervisory boards a generally significant source of information for the bank concerned: this is largely because of the ethical stance taken within the banks towards the use of information gained in this way.

Nor is the housebank concept prevalent – larger companies, i.e. those with turnovers in excess of DM500 million, were found to have in excess of ten active bank connections, and even the smallest companies had between two and five active bank connections. Competition among banks for corporate business is, in fact, fierce. It is more likely that banking relationships will be shared among several banks, with the one with the longest-standing connection taking the role of lead banker in syndicated business.

It is also clear that, unlike in Japan, German banks do not usually get involved in corporate reorganisations at operational management levels, and do not possess any specialists at turning round unprofitable companies. The main reasons for this appear to be that there is a strong convention that bank and industrial management are separate and distinct and that the direct involvement of a bank in a corporate rescue could raise liability questions for the bank should the rescue fail.

The area wherein the research did indicate there to be some truth in commonly held perceptions was that of bank control of equity voting rights. It has been estimated that German bank direct equity shareholding levels were at the level of 10.3 per cent in 1984 and 11.6 per cent in 1988, and that only in a small minority of cases were the banks able to exercise control as a result of their own shareholdings. Owing to the fact, however, that German shares are unregistered bearer shares, which are commonly deposited with the banks by small shareholders for custody and administration purposes, the banks (who are bound to consult with the beneficial owners) are able to exercise the votes of these shares on a proxy basis.

As the larger corporations tend to have the most widely dispersed shareholdings, and therefore likely to have the largest number of proxy votes, it is in this area that the banks appear to exercise the most control. In 30 cases out of the largest 100 industrial corporations, bank holdings, together with their committed proxy votes, were found to control in excess of 50 per cent of the votes available, while in a further 11 cases the combined vote was above 25 per cent, sufficient to block a resolution requiring a 75 per cent majority. Also, the bank vote is concentrated in the hands of the big three banks, namely Deutsche Bank, Dresdner Bank and Commerzbank, a fact which indicates an enormous concentration of power.

Such an enormous power base leads, of course, to large-scale participation as shareholder representatives on supervisory boards. In Aktiengesellschaft (AG), with more than 2000 employees, one half of the supervisory board membership must consist of employee representatives, with the other half being representatives of the shareholders – but the most important requirement is that the chairman of the board is elected by the shareholder representatives and has the right to cast a second vote in cases of board deadlock. Bank representatives hold a significant proportion of positions as supervisory board chairmen, in many cases even where they do not have majority voting control, either alone or with proxy votes.

The supervisory board has as its main function, according to the Aktiengesetz (Stock Corporation Act), the control of management: in this capacity it has the power to appoint and dismiss members of the management board (Vorstand) and to fix their remuneration. There is evidence, however, which casts doubts on the extent to which supervisory boards are capable of monitoring the activities of the management board: a 1988 study found that the vast majority of supervisory boards taking part in a study (86 per cent) met for only the legal minimum of twice a year, obviously too seldom to be able to provide any meaningful input to corporate decision-making.

In any event, the claim that, at the macro-level, the bank voting power is a reasonable representation of the public will, and therefore a force for encouraging management accountability, must itself be called into question: the banks themselves are AGs, and as such have a management board, a supervisory board and a chairman elected by the shareholders – but the banks, in an anacronistic twist of the system, also hold and can exercise proxy votes at their own general meetings, thus giving them, effectively, control of themselves! A recent estimate of the proxy votes held by the big three at their own shareholders' meetings was Deutsche Bank 47.2 per cent, Dresdner Bank 59.3 per cent and Commerzbank 30.3 per cent. So where is the incentive for the banks to act as shareholders' representatives elsewhere and a force for improved corporate accountability in general?

There are clearly many anomalies and inconsistencies in the German system of accountablitity, and it must also be borne in mind that the extent of shareholding in Germany is much smaller than in the UK, which again might encourage a less accountable approach from managers and institutions.

In an interesting parallel to the already-perceived characteristics of governance systems, Puxty et al. (1987), in discussing modes of regulation of accountancy in advanced capitalist societies, make use of Streeck and Schmitter's exploration of models of social order, which uses a combination of the organising principles of market, state and community.

In this paradigm, the UK is classed as principally associationist, being located between market and state, with important influences from both. Germany, on the other hand, is perceived as largely being influenced by the state and therefore being legalist in form. Both these interpretations could as easily be applied to the countries' governance and accountability systems.

References

- Edwards, JSS and Fischer, K (1991), 'An overview of the German financial system', Research paper.
- Jensen, MC (1989), 'Eclipse of the public corporation', *Harvard Business Review*, September/October.
- Monks, RAG and Minnow, N (1991), *Power and Accountability*, HarperCollins, New York.
- Nobes, C and Parker, R (1991), *Comparative International Accounting*, Prentice-Hall, London.
- Puxty, AG, Willmott, HC, Cooper, DJ and Lowe, T (1987), 'Modes of regulation in advanced capitalism: locating accountancy in four countries', *Accounting, Organizations and Society*, 12 (3), 273–91.
- Rappaport, A (1990), 'The staying power of the public corporation', *Harvard Business Review*, January/February
- Tricker, RI (1990), 'The corporate concept – redesigning a successful system'. *Human Systems Management*, 9, 65–76.

Further reading

- Monks, RAG and Minow, N (1995), *Corporate Governance*, Blackwell, Cambridge, Mass.
- Cannon, T (1994), *Corporate Responsibility*, Pitman Publishing, London.
- Smith, D (ed.) (1993), *Business and the Environment: Implications of the New Environmentalism*, Paul Chapman, London.
- Watts, RL and Zimmerman, JL (1983), 'Agency problems, auditing and the theory of the firm: some evidence', *Journal of Law and Economics*, XXVI, 613–33.
- Watts, RL and Zimmerman, JL (1986), *Positive Accounting Theory*, Prentice-Hall, Englewood Cliffs, NJ.
- Welford, R and Gouldson, A (1993), *Environmental Management and Business Strategy*, Pitman, London.

References

- Apostolou, B and Alleman F, *Internal Audit Briefings: Internal Audit Sampling*, Institute of Internal Auditors (USA) (1991).
- Auditing Practices Board, *The Future Development of Auditing: A Paper to Promote Public Debate*, November (1992).
- Auditing Practices Board, *Disclosures Relating to Corporate Governance* (revised) 1995/1, February (1995).
- Auditing Practices Board, *Internal Financial Control Effectiveness: A Discussion Paper*, April (1995).
- Beale, I and Bradford, R H, *Managing the Internal Audit: A Practical Handbook*, Kogan Page (1993).
- Beaumont and Sutherland, *Information Resources Management*, Butterworth-Heinemann (1992).
- Buttery, R, Hurford, C and Simpson, R K, *Audit in the Public Sector*, ICSA Publishing (2nd edn, 1993).
- CIMA, *Management Accounting: Official Terminology* (revised 1996).
- CIMA, *A Framework for Internal Control*, CIMA Law and Parliamentary Committee.
- CIMA, *Control in the Computer Environment*
- Chambers, A, *Effective Internal Audits: How to Plan and Implement*, Financial Times/Pitman (1992).
- Chambers, A D and Court, J M, *Computer Auditing*, Pitman (3rd edn, 1991).
- Chambers, A and Rand, G, *Auditing the IT Environment*, Financial Times/Pitman (1994).
- Chambers A, Selim and Vinten G, *Internal Auditing*, Pitman (2nd edn, 1990).
- CIPFA (Chartered Institute of Public Finance and Accountancy), *Computer Audit Guidelines*, CIPFA (4th edn, 1994).
- Comer, Michael J, *Corporate Fraud*, McGraw-Hill (2nd edn).
- Committee on the Financial Aspects of Corporate Governance, *Report of the Committee on the Financial Aspects of Corporate Governance*, Gee (1992).
- Dittenhofer, M A and Klemm, R J, *Ethics and the Internal Auditor*, Institute of Internal Auditors (USA) (1983).
- Douglas I J, *Computer Audit and Control Handbook*, Butterworth-Heinemann (1995).
- *Economist* (supplement), 'Watching the boss: a survey of corporate governance', 29 January (1994).
- Ernst & Young, *Corporate governance: Cadbury Implementation* (January, 1994).

- Ernst & Young, *Corporate governance: reporting on internal financial control* (April, 1995).
- Guy, D M, Carmichael, D R and Whittington, O R, *Audit Sampling: An Introduction*, Wiley (3rd edn, 1994).
- Hinde, S and Bentley, D F, 'Internal audit – an aid to management', *Accountants' Digest* 242, ICAEW (1990).
- Humphries G and Shaw-Taylor B, 'Statistical process control', *Management Accounting* (January, 1996).
- ICAEW, *Internal Control and Financial Reporting: Draft Guidance for Directors of Listed Companies*, ICAEW (1993).
- ICAEW, *Internal Control and Financial Reporting: Guidance for Directors of Listed Companies Registered in the UK*, ICAEW (December, 1994).
- ICAS, *Corporate Governance – Directors' Responsibility for Financial Statements* (1992).
- Institute of Internal Auditors (UK), *Audit Committees of the Board*, Professional Briefing Note 4 (1994).
- Institute of Internal Auditors (UK), *Internal Control*, Professional briefing note 6 (1994).
- Lothian, Niall, *Measuring Corporate Performance*, CIMA (1987).
- McRae, T W, *Statistical Sampling for Audit and Control*, Wiley (1974).
- Mills, RW and Kennedy JA, *Post-completion Audit of Capital Expenditure Projects*, Management Accounting Guide 9, CIMA (1990).
- Neale, C W, 'The Benefits Derived from Post-Auditing Investment Projects', *Omega*, Vol. 19, No. 23 (1991).
- Neale, Bill and Holmes, David, *Post-completion Auditing: A Guide for Effective Re-evaluation of Investment Projects*, Pitman (1991).
- Peabody, 'Perceptions of Organisational Authority', *Administrative Science Quarterly* (1962).
- Power, M, 'The Audit Society' in Hopwood A G and Miller P (eds), *Accounting as Social and Institutional Practice*, Cambridge (1994).
- Power, M, *The Audit Explosion*, Demos (1994).
- Price Waterhouse, *Value for Money Auditing: The Investigation of Economy, Efficiency, Effectiveness*, Gee & Co. (1990).
- Ratcliff, R L, Wallace, W A, Loebbecke, J K and McFardland, W G, *Internal Auditing: Principles and Techniques*, Institute of Internal Auditors (USA) (1988).
- Sawyer, L B, *Sawyer's Internal Auditing: The Practice of Modern Internal Auditing*, Institute of Internal Auditing (USA) (3rd edn, 1988).
- Sheridan and Kendall, *Corporate Governance*, Pitman (1992).
- Stearn, J and Impey, K, *Manual of Internal Audit Practice*, ICSA (1990).
- Travis B J, *Auditing the Development of Computer Systems*, Butterworths (1987).
- Venables J S R and Impey, K W, *Internal Audit*, Butterworths (1991)
- Vinten, G, 'Modern Internal Auditing' in Sherer, M and Turley, S (eds), *Current Issues in Auditing*, Paul Chapman Publishing (2nd edn, 1991).
- Weber, M, *The Theory of Social and Economic Organisation*, Free Press (1947), translated and edited by A M Henderson and T Parsons, extract from Pugh, *Organisation Theory*.

Index